THE
SHOTGUN
ENCYCLOPEDIA

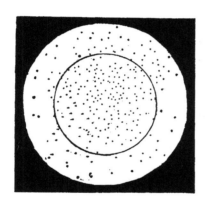

THE SHOTGUN ENCYCLOPEDIA

A Comprehensive Reference Work on All Aspects of Shotguns and Shotgun Shooting

by
John M. Taylor

To Tom —
A great guy and straight
shooter,

John Taylor

SAFARI PRESS INC.

Taylor, John M.

First edition

Safari Press Inc.

2001, Long Beach, California

ISBN 1-57157-165-5

Library of Congress Catalog Card Number: 99-68534

10 9 8 7 6 5 4 3 2 1

Readers wishing to receive the Safari Press catalog, featuring many fine books on big-game hunting, wingshooting, and sporting firearms, should write to Safari Press Inc., P.O. Box 3095, Long Beach, CA 90803, USA. Tel: (714) 894-9080 or visit our Web site at www.safaripress.com.

Dedication

To my dad, Curtis Taylor, who showed me what fun shotgunning could be, and who always took the time to take me hunting. And to the women in my life: Peggy, who always encouraged me, and somehow didn't let my flights into fantasy, when it came to shotguns I couldn't live without, destroy the family budget; and to Christine and Amy, who cheered for their dad at duck calling contests, and who grew up on the edges of skeet fields. May this not be all that I leave them.

Acknowledgments

The author and publisher wish to thank the following people for their contributions, without which this book would not have been possible.

Cyril Adams
Robert Anderson
Dr. William F. Andrews
ATA Trapshooting Hall of Fame
Colonel Craig Boddington
Sandra Boxdorfer
Robert S. Braden
Bob Brister
Browning
Connecticut Shotgun Mfg. Company
Dakota Arms Inc.
Antony Galazan
David Grant
Tom Henshaw
Griffin & Howe
Holland & Holland
Marvin Huey
Bob Hunter
Michael W. Jordan
Don Masters
Ed Muderlak
William Powell & Son (Gunmakers)
Ralph Stuart
Douglas Tate
David Trevallion
Upper Bay Museum, Northeast, Maryland
U.S. Repeating Arms Co./Winchester
Vic Venters
Weatherby
Winchester Division/Olin Industries

Foreword

There was a time when most American shooters needed to know two things about a shotgun: its price and how to take it apart to clean it. But this is the twenty-first century, and guns and shooters are becoming more sophisticated. Newcomers are confronted with myriad foreign and domestic gun designs, types of action, trigger mechanisms, and aftermarket enhancements. They hear about these things in gun stores or read about them in magazines, often without a clue to what all this means.

The game of Sporting Clays alone attracts some four million shooters a year, some of whom have never fired a shotgun. This game, which originated in England, has spawned its own language for the latest mechanical adaptations and advancements that simply make guns easier and more pleasant to hit with.

Now great numbers of shooters need a handy source for looking up terms like backboring and choke constriction. And if you are reading the foreign books and magazines that are popular with serious shotgunners, there are a lot of foreign terms for gun parts and such. These are also defined in this book.

It can be interesting just to read through this book, discovering words, items, and designs most shooters don't even know exist. If you've ever wondered exactly how your gun works, which part does what and why, most likely you will find the answers here, clearly and concisely stated and in many instances explained in detail.

John Taylor is well qualified to edit such an encyclopedia. He is technically oriented, knows shotguns inside and out, and is a tireless researcher. He is a lifelong hunter and shooter and is a master duck caller who has judged the world duck-calling championship several times. For more than a decade he was an Eastern Shore waterfowl guide. He has hunted from Canada to Africa and is an excellent shot, having qualified as a finalist for the 1975 Pan American Games and the 1976 Olympic skeet teams. He served in the U.S. Army for twenty-one years and retired with many awards and decorations. He is a contributing editor of the National Rifle Association's *American Rifleman* and *American Hunter* as well as *Petersen's Hunting.*

I've known John for years and have been impressed with his honesty and careful attention to detail. I believe you'll find his book to be complete and accurate and also easy to read and understand.

Bob Brister
Houston, Texas
1999

Introduction

There are several general firearms encyclopedias that have been in and out of print over the past thirty years. But nowhere is there an encyclopedia solely about the shotgun. Some common terms apply to every firearm, and nearly every book about shotguns contains a small glossary. Even common terms, however, often appear in a different light when they refer to shotguns. When Ludo Wurfbain approached me about doing this encyclopedia, I was both elated and terrified. There was so much to define, and so much that was veiled in history, lore, and legend. Once I'd begun the task, the flow of terms became an avalanche. One led to another and that to a further reference. The marvels of the computer and word-processing software have made my job easier—still, I may have overlooked some terms. If so, my apologies.

Because the British have such strong ties to shotguns and shotgunning, I've tried to include British terminology alongside the terms in common use in North America. As Americans, we are a nation of riflemen; the British, a nation of shotgunners. British shooting schools have greatly influenced the new generation of American shotgun enthusiasts, and thus it is proper that I clarify British shotgun terminology in this volume. I have also included terms from other languages that one might encounter in a catalog or elsewhere, as well as proof marks. Proof marks are particularly valuable when dealing with double guns. Often a vintage side-by-side will bear the name of a well-known London maker, yet the proof marks may show that the gun was in fact a product of, say, Birmingham. Proof marks tell volumes about the history of a firearm. Study them carefully if you are considering the purchase of a particular shotgun, or simply want to trace its lineage.

Insofar as manufacturers are concerned, I've included only those that I consider historically significant or that are currently producing shotguns. There are already many fine books about gun manufacturers; Geoffrey Boothroyd, Douglas Tate, and others have produced wonderful volumes on gunmakers. The subject is simply beyond the scope of this encyclopedia. In that same vein, I would encourage the reader to investigate the bibliography as carefully as the text. Listed there are excellent books full of information that expands on and complements what I have presented here. Many of the books are out of print, so I would urge those whose appetite I've whetted to check with used-book stores or the Internet.

Preface

This encyclopedia would not exist but for the kindness of my dear friend and colleague Col. Craig Boddington, U.S. Marine Corps Reserve. He graciously turned Ludo Wurfbain in my direction. Craig is one of the great editors and authors in outdoor and gun journalism, and he helped, directed, and guided me as I wrote for *Petersen's Hunting*. I might even have worked for him if we hadn't both been frozen in time during Operation Desert Storm. When a marine colonel told an army master sergeant (albeit now retired) that he ought to write a book, my only answer was a swift, "Yes sir!"

Once I'd begun this project I found it exhilarating, but also frustrating. I would come to a term, knowing that I had a reference for it, but where? Several individuals repeatedly came to my aid.

Douglas Tate, a through-and-through Britisher whom I first met on a duck, pigeon, and perdiz trip to Uruguay, patiently read my list of some seven hundred terms—there are now many more—and graciously suggested additions. Without his kindness, this encyclopedia would be incomplete. John Zent, the current editor of *American Hunter* and my boss during the three years I worked there, taught me how to write cleanly, to keep to the subject, and much more. He's one of the great editors in the business today, and I am indebted to him for teaching me how to write and edit.

Whenever I got stuck, my good friend Mike Jordan, manager of public affairs and public relations at the Winchester Division of the Olin Corporation, was there with advice. One of the greats in the arms and ammunition business, and one of the finest shotgunners in the world, Mike was always available to help, offer suggestions, and keep me on track.

Finally, my friend of twenty-five years, Robert N. Sears, offered his expertise. After I thought everything was about done, Bob had the good nature to read my manuscript. Bob Sears was for many years the technical editor of *American Rifleman*, and he has worked for many arms manufacturing companies along the way. You can hand Bob any kind of firearm in a soft case, and he can tell you what it is just by the feel. Having that kind of knowledge in my corner was an indescribable help.

To Doug, John, Mike, and Bob—my most heartfelt thanks. The mistakes are mine alone, but without your advice and counsel, there would, no doubt, have been many more.

THE
SHOTGUN
ENCYCLOPEDIA

Action: *The six basic styles of shotgun action.* **(Left to right)** *Single barrel; side-by-side; over/under; pump; gas-operated semiautomatic; and recoil-operated semiautomatic.*

Action: *Mass-produced side-by-side actions await further machining in a Spanish gun factory.*

Abercrombie and Fitch — One of the most famous outfitters in the United States (founded 1891), with showrooms in New York and Chicago. Their gun rooms were impressive, and many African safaris and other hunting expeditions were outfitted by them. Over the years Abercrombie and Fitch imported many shotguns for the American market. Sometime after World War II, Abercrombie and Fitch acquired the Chicago firm of Von Lengerke & Antoine, better known as V. L. & A., and their combined store operated for some time under both names, eventually becoming simply Abercrombie and Fitch. In 1976, Abercrombie and Fitch closed its doors, although recently it has reopened under the same name, selling only fashionable clothing.

Abbiatico & Salvinelli — Gardone, Italy. Manufacturer of extremely high-quality side-by-side and over/under shotguns. Only fifty to sixty are produced yearly, including a .410-bore four-barrel shotgun.

Abzug (Ger.) — "Trigger." See **trigger.**

Action — **1.** The portion of the shotgun that contains the firing mechanism or locks and to which the barrels and stock are attached. **2.** The style of the shotgun—that is, pump, semiautomatic, single-barrel, over/under, or side-by-side. See **receiver.**

Action bar — **1.** The linkage between the gas piston assembly and the slide that carries the breechbolt in a semiautomatic shotgun. The action bar transmits the rearward force of the gas piston and can be in the form of long flat bars or a long sleeve terminating in a short, round rod that impinges against the bolt carrier plate. **2.** The connecting bar or rod in a pump-action shotgun that transmits the force of the sliding fore-end to the action, opening and cycling it.

Action body — The part of the shotgun that carries the firing mechanism.

Action face — In a double shotgun, the flat section of the breech that is slightly less than 90 degrees upright from the action floor or flats. It is against the action face that the barrels come into battery. The cartridges rest against the action face, and at ignition the cartridge heads recoil against it. A shotgun is said to be "off the face" if its barrels no longer tightly abut and seal against the action face. See **breakoff, detonating, false breech, standing breech.**

Action flats — The area of a single-barrel, side-by-side, or over/under shotgun that is at a right angle to the action face and upon which the barrel flats lie when the gun is in battery. Manufacturers place proof marks, trademarks, and other pertinent information upon these action flats during manufacture.

Action size — In the conception and manufacture of shotguns, many makers provide frames appropriate to the gauge of gun. Not only doubles but also many pumps and semiautomatic shotguns have reduced or enlarged actions appropriate to their gauge.

Adjustable choke — A mechanical device that enables the shooter to control the pattern spread. Two of the most common devices are the Cutts Compensator and the Poly Choke. Current trends in shotgun design tend to use individual interchangeable, screw-in choke tubes. See **choke tubes, Cutts Compensator, Poly Choke.**

Air rifle training, United States Army — During the Vietnam conflict, United States Army recruits practiced hitting moving targets and shotgun-style shooting using air rifles and metal disks that fellow recruits launched as targets.

Amateur Trapshooting Association (ATA) — The North American organization that represents and regulates trapshooting. Established in 1923, it numbered 102,000 members in 1998. Amateur Trapshooting Association, 601 National Road, Vandalia, OH 45377.

American Arms, Inc. — Kansas City, Missouri, importer of various shotguns.

Amorce (Fr.) — "Primer." See **primer.**

Anson & Deeley action — The most commonly found boxlock action. This action received a patent on 11 May 1875, being the work of William Anson and John Deeley, both then employed by Westley Richards, the famous Birmingham gunmakers. It employs internal hammers that cock with the opening or fall of the barrels; as described in the patent, cocking "is effected by the rising of the breech ends of the barrels for charging." Although it became commonplace in the twentieth century, in 1875—still the age of the exposed-hammer shotgun—this action was a startlingly new concept in shotgun design. See **boxlock.**

Antirust rope — A tight-fitting cotton rope that, when soaked in oil, pulled into the bore of a shotgun, and left there, would supposedly protect the bore from rust during storage. In fact, the oil from ropes often ran out into the action; the rope then absorbed moisture and became solidly rusted into the bore, resulting in significant corrosion and damage.

Arcaded fences — A style of engraving, found on the fences or balls of the action of a side-by-side, that features arches enclosing small scroll engraving. Sometimes called umbrella-style engraving because the arches resemble opened umbrellas. (See illustration on page 6.)

Arrieta, S. L. — Elgoibar, Spain. A maker of high-quality side-by-sides. Several U.S. companies import Arrieta shotguns, which are made to individual order.

Arrizablaga, Pedro — Eibar, Spain. Maker of best-quality bespoke shotguns since 1940. Many consider them the Purdey of Spain.

Articulated trigger — The front trigger of a double-trigger shotgun, constructed so that it will pivot forward during recoil so as not to strike the shooter's trigger finger. Normally, only the

Arcaded fences: *The arcaded fences shown here were typical of the London best Woodward guns. Also illustrated is the extended bearing surface for the tumbler (hammer) axle, which projects slightly from the side plate.*

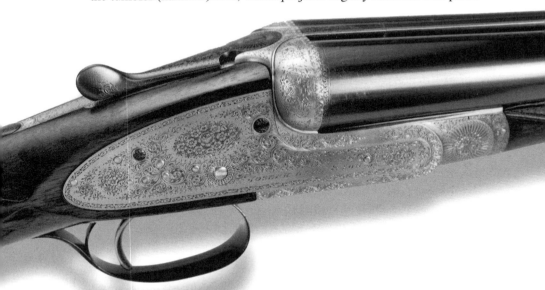

Beaded Fences: *Fences may be defined as the juncture between the flat surface of the action body and the rounded hemispheres (balls) of the action that close off the breech end of the barrels. Pictured here are beaded fences.*

more expensive side-by-sides have an articulated trigger, but occasionally manufacturers will build the device into over/unders, most of which today have single triggers.

August 12 — The "Glorious Twelfth," the traditional opening date of the red grouse season in Scotland. During the Edwardian era, this date marked the opening of the shooting season and the flurry of highly structured, social shooting parties that ensued. Even today, highly structured although less formal rules from the nineteenth century still govern driven shooting. See **etiquette.**

Auswerfer (Ger.) — "Ejector." See **ejectors.**

Auszieher (Ger.) — "Extractor." See **extractors.**

Autoloader — A semiautomatic firearm that, when the trigger is pulled, fires the chambered round, then opens the action, extracts and ejects the fired hull or shell, and chambers a fresh round. The best example of autoloading by recoil operation is the Browning Automatic-5 shotgun, which locks the barrel and breechbolt together until both have recoiled fully to the rear of the action. The bolt is then grabbed and held as a powerful spring that surrounds the magazine tube thrusts the barrel forward. As the barrel goes forward, the extractor holds the fired shell to the face of the breechbolt; when the barrel is nearly fully forward, the two-pronged ejector at the rear of the barrel extension ejects the fired hull (see **barrel extension**). At this moment, the bolt is released.

As the bolt travels forward it trips the carrier, which rises, bringing with it a new shell from the magazine. The carrier aligns the unfired shell with the chamber, and the bolt pushes it home. The extractor then slips over the rim, and the cycle is ready to repeat. When the last shot has been fired, the bolt remains locked to the rear, keeping the gun safe and indicating to the shooter that the shotgun is empty.

Autoloading can also be accomplished through the use of expanding propellant gases. Gas-operated semiautomatic shotguns have one or two ports drilled through the barrel, some five to nine inches from the end of the chamber. When the gun fires, the expanding gases bleed off through the port and strike the gas piston. As the piston drives rearward it imparts movement to the heavier action bars and thus to the slide, which drives rearward, unlocking the breechbolt from

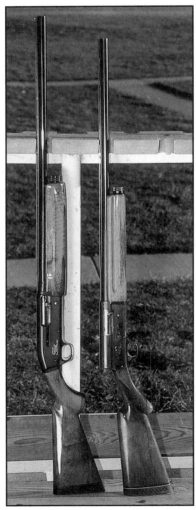

Autoloader: (Left) *The Browning Gold gas-operated semiautomatic, which functions by bleeding off a small amount of the propellant gas.* **(Right)** *The venerable Browning Automatic 5, which uses the force of recoil to operate its action.*

Safari Press, America's premier sporting publisher, regularly releases books on worldwide big-game hunting, wingshooting, and sporting firearms. Please complete and return this postcard and you will be updated on our new publications. *(Please do not send this post card if you have previously received a book from Safari Press; you are already on our mailing list.)*

PLEASE PRINT:

NAME _____

ADDRESS _____

CITY/STATE _____ ZIP _____

COUNTRY _____ TEL (___) ____ - ____

PLACE POSTAGE HERE

SAFARI PRESS INC.

P.O. Box 3095

Long Beach, CA 90803-0095, USA

the barrel extension and pushing the bolt and carrier to the rear. The bolt goes rearward, and the extractor mounted on the outboard side of the bolt extracts the fired hull. As the bolt ends its rearward travel, the ejector, normally a pin or other protrusion mounted on the inside of the receiver, ejects the hull. At the end of its rearward travel, the bolt trips the magazine latch, releasing a fresh shell. (If there is no shell in the magazine, the bolt is latched to the rear.) When a fresh round enters the action from the magazine, it trips the bolt release, allowing the bolt to travel forward. As the bolt goes forward it activates the carrier dog, a cam device that lifts the carrier and the fresh shell into alignment with the chamber. The forward-moving bolt pushes the round into the chamber, and the extractor slips over the rim of the fresh shell. See **action, receiver**.

Automatic — A term misapplied to, and often confused with, the term *semiautomatic*. A fully automatic firearm is one capable of continuous fire without releasing the trigger. A semiautomatic firearm requires that the shooter pull the trigger for each shot.

"The Automatic" James Woodward — An early breechloading shotgun or double rifle developed by Woodward. This gun, in either shotgun or rifle configuration, used an underlever that lay against the forward portion of the trigger guard to open the barrels and cock the hammers or tumblers. Depending upon the extent to which the lever was extended, the tumblers could be brought either to half-cock or full cock—by then an anachronism, since this gun was primarily built as a hammerless action. Hammer guns were also available, however. In parallel development with the Anson & Deeley action—introduced in 1875, the year prior to the introduction of The Automatic—Woodward adopted the Purdey-style underbolt and top lever. However, they continued to use the trade name "Automatic" as late as 1923, especially in relation to their double rifles, which were available with either a top lever or an underlever.

Automatic ejector — A device specific to the over/under, side-by-side, and some single-barrel shotguns. Following firing and upon opening of the gun, a spring-loaded plunger or hammer throws the spent hulls free of the chamber by driving the extractor upward. Shotguns with selective automatic ejectors depend upon the firing of the individual barrels to trip the ejector. If a barrel remains unfired, the cam action of the extractor toe lifts the unfired shells above the level of the breech end of the barrel to facilitate removal.

Automatic safety — The safety catch on an over/under or side-by-side that moves to the ON-SAFE position whenever the shotgun is opened. Most use a simple linkage activated by the top lever that pushes the safety catch rearward into the ON position whenever the lever is rotated. See **top lever.**

AyA (Aguirre y Aranzabal) — Eibar, Spain. In business since 1915, AyA has produced a variety of side-by-side and over/under shotguns in both sidelock and boxlock configurations. During the 1980s they became part of the ill-fated Diarm, a Basque/Spanish government-formed consortium that lasted only a year or two. Now independently owned, AyA manufactures quality British-style shotguns, which they export mainly to Great Britain and Europe.

AyA: An exterior view of the Aguirre y Aranzabal factory in Eibar, Spain.

AyA: A workman in the AyA factory checks a barrel for straightness and finish.

Back action — A style of sidelock shotgun in which the action mainspring lies behind the hammers.

Backboring — Also called overboring, backboring is the technique of slightly enlarging the interior bore of a shotgun beyond the normal dimensions. In the 12-bore shotgun, the nominal SAAMI standard bore diameter is 0.729 inch; backboring normally enlarges the bore to about 0.740. The benefits are denser and more evenly distributed patterns; some also feel there is a reduction of recoil. See **overboring, SAAMI.**

Baker, Stan — A Seattle, Washington, gunsmith who pioneered aftermarket screw-in chokes. Using a proprietary method, Baker expanded the muzzle area of single-barrel and some over/under barrels so they could be threaded to accept interchangeable choke tubes.

Balance — The distribution of weight in a shotgun. A shotgun for game shooting that possesses good balance is said to have 50 percent of the weight between the hands, 25 percent in the buttstock, and 25 percent in the barrels. Shotguns intended for target shooting have more weight toward the muzzle. Many otherwise well-designed shotguns, such as the Browning Double Automatic and the Winchester Models 50 and 59, failed because of their poor, butt-heavy balance.

Ball trap — See **glass ball traps.**

Balls — Another term for fences, the two spheres that top the action of a side-by-side or over/under and mate with the barrels. See **fences.**

Bank note engraving — See **bulino.**

Bar — Also called the action bar, this is the projection from the action face that holds the hinge pin and against which the barrels lie when in battery. See **battery, in; hinge pin.**

Bar action — A sidelock action in which the mainspring lies in front of the tumbler. See also **back action.**

Bar-in-wood — A form of action body in which the buttstock wood goes up to the hinge pin on the underside and the action bar is very thin.

Barker Gun and Forging Co. — Located in Batavia, New York, Barker made side-by-side shotguns from 1889 to 1933, when the company fell victim to the Great Depression.

Bar lock — A type of sidelock in which the mainspring is in front of the hammer. It takes its name from the fact that the mainspring is inletted into the action bar. See **action bar, sidelock.**

Barrel — The tube that contains and directs the shot toward the target. Working forward from the breech end: The chamber is the portion of the barrel that holds the unfired shell; the very end of the barrel is rebated to accommodate the shell rim. Immediately forward of the chamber is the chamber forcing cone, which provides a smooth transition for the ejecta—propellent gases, wad, and shot—from the wider chamber into the cylindrical portion of the barrel. Beginning from three to seven inches from the muzzle is the choke-forcing cone, which starts the transition from the bore to the choke. Finally, the choke shapes the shot charge. Varying in constriction from none (or "straight cylinder") to a maximum of about 0.05 inch, the choke constricts the tube, either to tighten the shot charge or to shape it. Exterior barrel features may include a front bead to provide orientation, a ventilated or solid rib, the manufacturer's name, various patent numbers, proof marks, locking lugs or recesses, barrel extension, and extractor/ejector blades. (See illustrations on pages 11, 14.) See **barrel extension, chamber, choke, ejector, extractor, forcing cone, locking lugs, proof marks, rib, sights.**

Barrel extension — A hardened-steel extension threaded into the rear of the barrel of a pump or semiautomatic shotgun that provides the cuts that engage the breechbolt locking block. In addition, the barrel extension frequently carries the ejector stud, which throws the extracted hull free of the action. Because the locking

Barrel: *This side-by-side barrel shows its chopper lumps, concealed third fastener, the mating surface for the side clips, and fore-end loop.*

Barrel: *Partially finished over/under barrels awaiting final machining.*

block engages the barrel extension, all of the forces of recoil and pressure are taken by this assembly, frequently allowing the use of lightweight alloys in the construction of the receiver. See **breechbolt, locking block**.

Barrel flats — The flat area under the breech end of the barrels of a side-by-side that mates with the water table or action flats when the shotgun is closed or in battery. Barrel proof marks are most frequently on the barrel flats. See **battery, in; water table**.

Barrel lumps — Forged integral with either the barrels or the monobloc, these lumps or projections of metal become, after machining, the hook that engages the hinge pin or cross pin, and at the rear the locking recesses that receive the locking bolts or underbolt. See **cross pin, hinge pin, lump, monobloc, underbolt**.

Barrel selector — The means by which the shooter controls the firing order of a shotgun with two or more barrels but only one trigger. The selector is most commonly a small button either on the trigger or combined with the safety catch on the top strap. Pushing the selector in one direction or the other will determine which barrel fires first. Most shotgunners select the more open barrel and

Barrel selector: An in-trigger, button-style barrel selector.

fire it first, followed by the more tightly choked barrel. See **safety**.

Barrel separation — A problem that results when the barrels of a side-by-side or over/under become loose and are no longer in proper regulation. It may be the result of bulging in one or both barrels because the gun was fired with an obstruction present, or it may be the result of using steel shot in guns designed solely for lead. In other cases barrel separation can result when the ribs come loose, either because of poor initial assembly or subsequent damage. Barrel separation is often very costly to repair: It is necessary to disassemble the barrels completely, clean all of the parts, remove the bulge (if possible) or obtain and strike a new tube, reassemble the gun, reregulate it, and refinish the newly reconstructed barrels.

Barrel thickness — The thickness of the walls of a shotgun barrel. The British gun trade has no set standard, but seemingly the minimum is 0.02 inch for shotguns chambered for 2- and 2½-inch shells, and 0.025 inch and thicker for shotguns

Barrel thickness: *Joe Prather measures barrel thickness with a special measuring fork in the gun room of Griffin & Howe's New Jersey facility.*

chambered for 2¾-inch shells. American-made shotguns are normally overbuilt, and even the thinnest of barrels measures about 0.035 inch. With few exceptions, shotguns manufactured in Belgium, Germany, France, and Italy have equally thick barrels. When contemplating the purchase of a British-made shotgun or one with apparently thin barrels, it is wise to check their thickness. Measurement of barrel wall thickness should be done with a wall-thickness micrometer. These are expensive and are not often encountered in the United States, as the wall thickness on most American shotguns is not an issue. The devices are more common in Europe, where new barrels are made much thinner to begin with. See **fork**.

Battery (waterfowling) — **1.** In the early days of wildfowl or waterfowl hunting in the United States, when market

Battery: Anchored in the relatively shallow waters of the upper Chesapeake Bay, the battery floated level with the surface of the water and effectively concealed the gunner from approaching ducks. The decoys around the edge are of cast iron, being added or removed to provide ballast. Here Bob Litzenberg demonstrates shooting from a lay-down battery that is now on display in the Upper Bay Museum in North East, Maryland.

hunting was legal, hunters used large or multibarrel shotguns called battery guns. These large-bore or multiple-barrel guns were mounted to the front of a low-profile boat propelled by a single sculling oar. The quarry was large flocks of resting birds, often hunted at night. 2. A blind or hide, sometimes called a battery box, submerged to the point that the water just covered the decking that surrounded the box. Using a battery amid a large set of decoys makes the hunters invisible to the ducks until the hunter rises to fire. Once in extensive use on the tidal flats at the mouth of the Susquehanna River, where it flows into Chesapeake Bay, this style of hunting rig—along with battery and punt guns and night hunting—became illegal in the United States in the early years of the twentieth century. Battery box hunting still occurs on a very limited area of the St. Lawrence River in Quebec, Canada.

Battery, in — The position of the firing mechanism at the moment when a firearm is ready to fire, with the bolt fully home or the breech fully closed and locked against a chambered cartridge. The shooter then need only cock the hammer or move the safety catch to the fire position and pull the trigger.

Battue — A thin and extremely hard clay target in use in sporting clays and FITAS shooting. See **clay target, FITAS, sporting clays.**

Bead sight: Two types of bead sights. On right is the bead most commonly found, a single, simple steel bead. On left is one of the currently popular fiber-optic beads that seem to glow in low light.

Bead — 1. The front sight, positioned at the muzzle end of the barrel. 2. A thin line of engraving that sets off or emphasizes a particular part of a shotgun. See **sights**.

Beaded fences — A thin line of raised metal at the juncture of the flat sides of the action and the balls or hemispheres that engage the rear of the barrels. Action filers use beaded fences most commonly on side-by-side shotguns.

Beaded trigger guard — The thickening and rounding of the bottom edge of the trigger guard on the side nearest the trigger finger. This smooth surface provides a more comfortable resting place for the trigger finger while the hunter walks through cover, or at times when the finger rests on the guard close to but not touching the trigger.

Beavertail fore-end — 1. A widened and deepened fore-end clay shooters use to keep their fingers from contacting the hot barrels, and that positions the leading hand closer to the

Beavertail: An example of a beavertail fore-end as found on the Winchester Model 21.

center of the bore of the bottom barrel. 2. Any fore-end that is wider and deeper than the norm or the aesthetics of the shotgun dictates.

Bend (Brit.) — The dimensions of the buttstock that define the placement of the cheek. See **drop**.

Benelli — Urbino, Italy. Benelli imports its line of semiautoloading, pump, and over/under shotguns into the United States under the auspices of Beretta U.S.A.

Bent (Brit.) — The notch in the hammer or tumbler that the nose of the sear engages when the hammer is cocked. The half-bent notch is the half-cock position. See **sear notch**.

Beretta, Pietro — The world's oldest firearms manufacturer. Founded in 1529, Beretta manufactures a complete line of semiautomatic, over/under, and side-by-side shotguns. Imported and distributed in the United States by Beretta

Beretta: *Ugo Beretta (left), a direct descendant of the founding Beretta family, admires a shotgun made by his company.*

U.S.A., Beretta uses state-of-the-art manufacturing and quality-control equipment that creates high-volume production with equally high quality.

Bernadelli, Vincenzo — In business in Brescia, Italy, since 1721, Bernadelli makes semiautomatics, over/unders, side-by-sides, combination guns, and double rifles.

Bertuzzi — Located in Brescia, Italy, this firm produces only forty to fifty best-quality sidelock over/unders and side-by-sides a year.

Bespoke shotgun (Brit.) — A gun that purchasers order to their own specific and individual specifications. Such specifications include barrel length, pattern percentages with specified loads, a stock made to the customer's fitted measurements, and engraving. Each finished shotgun is unique to the purchaser.

Bicycle gun — See **folding shotgun**.

Bifurcated lumps — Often called trunnions, these are round buttonlike projections that are found on opposite sides of the lower barrel of an over/under and on which the barrels pivot. These bifurcated lumps fit into matching recesses in the frame. Italian over/under shotguns such as Perazzi and Beretta make use of a similar style of barrel pivot, but in the case of these shotguns, the parts are reversed with the trunnions projecting from the receiver sides and engaging rounded cuts machined into the sides of the barrels. See **lump**.

Bikal — Manufacturer of double shotguns in Izhevsk and Tula, Russia. Imports have been infrequent and subject to Russian-style marketing.

Bismuth shot — A type of nontoxic shot compliant with regulations forbidding the use of lead shot; used mainly for the taking of waterfowl. Previous to the development of bismuth shot, soft iron or steel shot was the only approved nontoxic shot. Bismuth is much closer to the weight and softness of lead, making it ballistically preferable to steel while at the same time making possible its use in shotguns whose barrels would be damaged by steel shot.

Bites (Brit.) — The cuts in the lumps that accept the locking bolt, which, when engaged in the bites, locks the barrels to the action of a double shotgun preparatory to and during firing. See **notch**.

Black game (Brit.) — The black grouse *(Lyrurus tetrix)* or, colloquially, black cock. Black grouse are later to mature

Black game: *The black grouse occurs throughout Europe and Asia. They are shot during drives (often as a target of opportunity during red grouse shoots) or at their lek in the spring. Once a common bird, they are now greatly reduced in number because of habitat destruction.*

than the more common red grouse. Hunters more often take them by walking up or during late-season drives. The black cock is the source of the lyre-shaped plume worn in the hat badge of some Highland regiments.

Blacking; Blackening (Brit.) — The finish applied to the metal parts of a shotgun; often called bluing. See **bluing**.

Blades (Brit.) — The trigger or triggers of a shotgun. See **trigger**.

Bleimeister process — Developed in Germany, this is a method of manufacturing shot using a short-drop process. It is a technique for creating the smaller-size bismuth pellets (larger sizes, No. 2, and BB are cast). In this method of pellet-making, the manufacturer pours molten lead or bismuth through a sieve precisely drilled to drop pellets of a specific size. The molten material drops about three feet into a water bath, which completes the hardening process. Because of its compact size, the Bleimeister machine will fit in virtually any factory setting—typically a warehouse; it does not require the 200-foot-high tower that manufacturers employ in the conventional production of shot.

Blind — A place of concealment for hunters from approaching waterfowl. Blinds can be as simple as a piece of camouflage netting draped over stakes or tree branches, or as elaborate as enclosed structures with roofs, electric lights, a kitchen, and an adjoining boat blind complete with ramps or steps leading into the main blind. Plywood is the most common building material for blinds, which may be permanently located on the shore

Blind: *These duck hunters are shooting from a pit that is blind dug into a dike surrounding a flooded soybean field.*

of a body of water, built on stakes out in the water, or built on the stumps of old trees or actually in trees. Some hunters use blinds on boats, employing folding panels that can make the boat look like a floating brush pile; some boats serve solely as blinds, being maneuvered into cover. Waterfowlers construct blinds in a nearly endless number of shapes and styles. See **butt, hide, pit**.

Blitz action (Ger.) — A style of shotgun action in which the firing mechanism, triggers, mainsprings, sears, and hammers are attached to the bottom plate and can be removed as a unit. Typical of this action are the Perazzi competition over/unders and the Dickson Round Action side-by-side, manufactured in Edinburgh, Scotland.

Blowback action — A type of semiautomatic action that relies upon a carefully calibrated spring and the weight of the breechbolt to resist the rearward force of the propellant gases on the breechbolt. This style of action is most common to semiautomatic pistols and to submachine guns.

Blue Book of Gun Values — A comprehensive listing of most contemporary and antique firearms, with brief histories of the various manufacturers, the dates of manufacture for specific models, and current market prices based on condition. Blue Book Publications, 8009 34th Avenue, Minneapolis, MN 55425; Phone 800-877-4867.

Blue pill — 1. A proof load. 2. An informal term applied to ammunition used in proof testing. See **proof load**.

Bluing — The finish applied to most metal surfaces of a shotgun. Bluing may be of two types, hot (or nitre) and cold (or rust) bluing. In either case, the first step is to completely degrease the metal. In the case of hot-bluing, there is a variety of solutions the gunmaker may use. Whatever the formulation of the solution, the gunmaker will bring it to a very high temperature before immersing the parts. After removal from the bluing solution, the parts are washed, then cured in oil.

Rust-bluing involves careful degreasing followed by the application of a solution of acids—there are many formulas, most of which are secret, proprietary concoctions. The gunmaker then places the barrels in a cabinet that provides high humidity and heat. Within a few hours, the barrels will display a fine covering of red rust. Boiling and carding or polishing follows, and the gunmaker repeats the entire process until the bluing is sufficiently deep. Traditionally, gunmakers use hot-bluing for pump-action, semiautomatic, and inexpensive single-barrel shotguns. The actions and furniture of over/unders and side-by-sides typically receive the same treatment. However, because fine double-barrel shotguns are traditionally joined by soldering, rust-bluing is necessary for the barrels of those guns. Makers of more contemporary double shotguns, such as the Ruger Red Label, employ mechanical joining and hot-bluing.

Bob-weight — Another term for the inertia block or pendulum used in a single trigger as applied to a double gun. During recoil, this weight or block disengages the sears, preventing the second barrel from firing until the recoil phase of the shot is concluded. See **inertia block**.

Bob-weight peg — The pin around which the bob-weight or inertia block swings.

Boca (Sp.) — "Muzzle."

Bocca (Ital.) — "Muzzle."

Boddington, Colonel Craig, USMCR — Primarily recognized as one of the foremost authorities on rifles and big-game hunting, Boddington, during his tenure as editor of *Petersen's Hunting* magazine, initiated and solicited many articles about shotgunning. For several years he coauthored with this author the monthly *Petersen's Hunting's* "Shotgunning" column, bringing to readers his own experiences and insights pertaining to the shotgun.

Bogardus, Capt. Adam H. — A prominent American shooting figure in the late 1800s. Reports have it that he shot 5,000 glass balls in 500 minutes and performed other such feats. In the opinion of author Bob Hinman in his book *The Golden Age of Shotgunning*, "If America were to name one all-time, all-round champion of the shotgun, a chief candidate would be Adam H. Bogardus. . . . The facts show he was a great shot in a time of great shooters."

Bolstered action — A side-by-side or over/under shotgun with the action specially reinforced along the fences and beneath the flats. Magnum wildfowling shotguns and large-caliber double rifles most often employ bolstered actions.

Bolt-action — An action style based upon the turn-bolt rifle action typified by those made by Mauser and Winchester. Although the bolt-action is an inexpensive shotgun to manufacture, the slowness of operating the bolt makes this style action a minor player. Few such guns use locking lugs similar to those found on a rifle's action, but instead lock up through engagement of the bolt handle with a cut in the action. While not inherently unsafe, because of the lower pressure generated by shotshells, some bolt-action shotguns are nevertheless suspect. Most recently, though, some high-quality, high-performance bolt-action shotguns have become available, solely for shooting sabot-encased slugs at big game, notably white-tailed deer. These bolt-action shotguns feature lapped locking lugs, precision-rifled barrels, receivers drilled for mounting telescopic sights, and bolt handles shaped to accommodate scopes. See **locking lugs, sabot**.

Boothroyd, Geoffrey — British gunwriter who has documented much of the history and lore of gunmaking in the United Kingdom.

Bore — The interior of the barrel.

Boring, gun barrel — In most instances, gunmakers bore shotgun barrels as a straight cylinder to the last eight inches with a deep-drilling or reaming machine. Three to five inches from the muzzle, the choke-forcing cone begins. The gunmaker then cuts the chamber and chamber-forcing cones, and, in the case of a bespoke shotgun, reams chokes by hand to a specific pattern percentage with a specified load. Mass-production shotguns often employ cold hammer-forged barrels formed over a mandrel whose exterior matches the interior dimensions of the finished barrel. Choking of mass-produced shotguns is based on the mathematical difference between the dimensions of the cylinder bore and a predetermined amount of choke constriction. See **chamber, choke, paradox gun**.

Boss & Company, London — Established in 1830, Boss and Company continues in business. In 1909, Boss patented their over/under shotgun. Although it was not the first of its kind, many rated it as one of the finest ever produced. Boss shotguns are among the finest in the world.

Boswell, Charles — Another of the old-line London gunmakers.

Bouche (Fr.) — "Muzzle."

Bouquet and scroll — A style of engraving.

Box birds — One of two forms of live pigeon shooting (the other being *colombarie*, in which the birds are thrown by a human thrower known as a *colombarie*). Pigeons fly from a collapsing box with a hinged top and sides. In competition, officials load five or more boxes or traps with pigeons at the start of each shooter's turn. On signal, one of the boxes collapses, and a blast of compressed air or electrical shock induces the bird to fly. In North America, spring traps are sometimes used, which throw the bird one to two feet straight up into the air. Shooters in America stand thirty to thirty-four yards from the traps; Europeans stand twenty-four to thirty meters from the release point. After release, the shooter must kill the bird before it crosses a low fence erected as close as twelve or fifteen yards from the traps, although seventeen yards is considered average. The rules allow two shots for each bird, and many competitions require that shooters fire both barrels as a safety measure to ensure that no one turns away from the firing position with an unfired round chambered. Participants wager great sums of money on individual shooters, birds, and any other permutation that generates odds and an opportunity to bet. See *colombarie,* **pigeon shooting**.

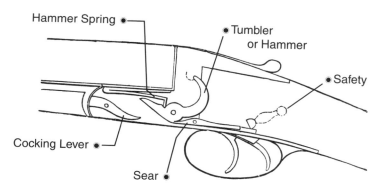

Boxlock — A shotgun action, perhaps the most popular action of all among makers of over/under and side-by-side shotguns. William Anson and John Deeley patented the most common of this style action on 11 May 1875. That action carries the triggers, sears, hammers, and all the attendant springs within the action body. Prior to the development of the Anson & Deeley action, shotguns had external hammers; evolving guns of the hammerless variety were of the sidelock design, which carries the sear and hammer on plates mounted on the sides of the action. Of great appeal in the Anson & Deeley boxlock was its simplicity and the fact that it uses the leverage of the opening barrels to cock the hammers. In the Anson & Deeley action, one end of the cocking lever projects from the action knuckle, and the other end goes back into the action body, where it contacts the cocking surface of the tumbler or hammer. Upon opening, cuts in the fore-end iron engage the cocking lever; as they rotate, the other end of the lever, using its great mechanical advantage, cocks the hammers. In regard to simplicity, the average sidelock has ten or more individual parts, the boxlock only four: the cocking lever, tumbler or hammer, sear, and mainspring. There are other styles of boxlock action, such as the Westley Richards drop lock and the German Blitz; the Anson & Deeley, however, in one modified form

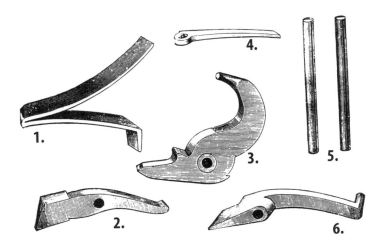

Boxlock action:
1. Mainspring or hammer/tumbler spring. 2. Cocking lever. 3. Tumbler or hammer and integral firing pin or striker. 4. Sear spring. 5. Pivot pins passing through action, around which the tumblers, sears, and cocking lever rotate. 6. Sear.

or another, remains the most popular. See **blitz action, droplock, knuckle, mainspring, sidelock tumbler**.

Breakoff (Brit.) — The part of the action that is at a right angle to the action bar through which the firing pins or strikers project and that houses the top lever. See **action face, detonating, standing breech**.

Break-top action — A shotgun in which rotating the barrels from the action face opens the action. Almost all single-barrel, side-by-side, and over/under shotguns are of this type.

Breech face — See **action face, breakoff, detonating, false breech, standing breech**.

Breech loading — Any firearm that loads by means of inserting a self-contained cartridge directly into the barrel's chamber.

Breechbolt — The part of the action in semiautomatic and pump-action shotguns that carries the firing pin and extractor

Breechbolt: *The breechbolt of a semiautomatic shotgun.*

and that locks to the frame or barrel extension, sealing the shell within the chamber.

Brenneke slug — A proprietary slug manufactured in Germany and intended for use on big game. In the Brenneke slug the wad material is securely attached to the base of the slug to provide better stability and accuracy. See **Foster slug, sabot, wad.**

Brescia, Italy — The major firearms manufacturing area in Italy.

Bridle — The large, decoratively shaped component of a sidelock that holds the hammer or tumbler so that it can rotate with a minimum of friction.

Briley, Jess — The Houston, Texas, gunsmith and founder of Briley Manufacturing who refined the development of the screw-in choke so that virtually any shotgun can now be accommodated. Briley's company is also known for manufacturing small-gauge insert tubes for use in double shotguns, whereby the shooter can quickly convert his shotgun to a smaller gauge by simply inserting an appropriately fitted tube into his larger-gauge barrels. Briley Manufacturing currently offers virtually all gunsmithing services that pertain to shotguns and currently furnishes screw-in chokes for the prestigious line of Holland & Holland over/under game guns.

Bob Brister

Brister, Robert ("Bob") — For many years shooting editor of *Field & Stream*. His book *Shotgunning: The Art and Science* is considered a classic.

British Association for Shooting and Conservation, The — One of the major British conservation organizations, the BASC dedicates its work to the furtherment of shooting. For information, contact BASC, Marford Mill, Rossett, Wrexham, Clwyd LL12 0HL, U.K.

British Field Sports Society, The — A British association that supports and promotes shooting. In the 1990s it was absorbed into Countryside Alliance.

Brno Arms — Manufacturing company in Brno and Uherski, Czech Republic. Makers of side-by-side, over/under, and combination guns.

Brown, David McKay — Established in 1967 in Glasgow, Scotland, Brown makes over/under and round action-style side-by-side shotguns in the manner of John Dickson &

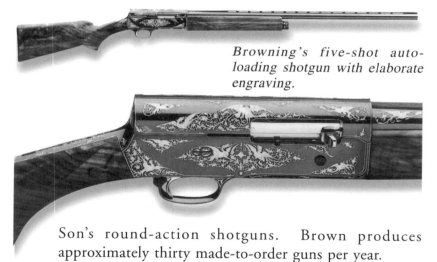

Browning's five-shot auto-loading shotgun with elaborate engraving.

Son's round-action shotguns. Brown produces approximately thirty made-to-order guns per year.

Browning — Founded by John Moses Browning, Browning has never manufactured firearms in its own facilities; instead, it has always been an importer. As such, the classic Automatic-5 shotgun was the work of either the Fabrique

Nationale (F.N.) factory in Belgium or (for later models) Japanese factories. Dropped from the Browning line in 1997, several million Auto-5s are still in use worldwide. Other shotguns made by Browning are the Superposed, the first mass-produced over/under shotgun. Today Browning features a full line of shotguns from hunting to competition in over/under (Citori or Superposed), pump (BPS), and gas-operated autoloader (Gold).

Browning, John Moses — (1855–1926) America's greatest gun designer. In addition to various highly successful military arms, John Moses Browning also developed the Browning Automatic-5 semiautomatic shotgun, the Winchester Models 1893 and 1897—later called the Model 97—

Browning, John Moses: *America's most prolific firearms designer.*

exposed-hammer pumps, the bottom-ejecting pump-action shotgun typified by the Remington 17 and the Ithaca 37, and others.

Bruchet, Paul — Located in St.-Étienne, France, this gunmaker is now producing the unique Darne shotgun. Paul Bruchet served as line foreman at Darne until the closing of the Darne plant in 1979. He manufactured Darne-style shotguns under his own name from 1981 until 1989, when he was able to retain the Darne trademark; subsequent manufacture has been under that trademark.

Brush load — A cartridge loaded in 12-gauge with special wads that produce a more open pattern when fired from a full-choked shotgun. These loads were popular during the era prior to World War II, when virtually all shotguns sold were full choke. Using these brush loads enabled the owner of a full-choked shotgun to shoot a pattern more appropriate for quail and other close-flushing upland game. Also called scatter loads.

Buckingham, Nash — (1880-1971) A well-known American outdoor writer of the first three-quarters of the twentieth century. Buckingham was famous for his excellent shotgun marksmanship and for his work in testing and

Buckingham, Nash: Nash shooting at Nilo Farms, Alton, Illinois. Photo by Robert S. Anderson from the collection of Dr. William F. Andrews.

developing magnum loads for waterfowl. His stories are nostalgic vignettes of quail and waterfowl hunting from the turn of the century through the late 1960s.

Buckshot — Large lead shotgun pellets commonly used to shoot big game such as white-tailed deer or when tracking wounded, thin-skinned, dangerous African game such as lion and leopard. Pellets are either numbered or given a letter designation to define size. In the United States, the smallest buckshot pellets are designated No. 4 and measure 0.24 inch in diameter. Pellet size increases as their numerical designation decreases through number one, measuring 0.30 inch, then 0 (aught) at 0.32 inch, to the largest, 000 (triple aught), measuring .36 inches. The most popular size of buckshot in America is 00, which measures 0.34 in diameter. British and European designations are alphabetical. Equivalent sizes are SSSG, 0.245 inch (U.S. No. 4), through SG (U.S. size 000). British buckshot sizes extend beyond U.S. sizes on the large end of the scale to LG, which measures 0.388 inch in diameter. Strictly a close-range proposition, buckshot should always be shot using full choke, and range should be limited to within 30 yards. Beyond 30 yards, the small number of pellets spread very widely, even when shot from a full-choked shotgun, and there are too few pellet strikes within the relatively small vital area of even a large deer—approximately eight inches—to ensure a clean kill.

Bulged barrel — Because shotgun barrels are of thin construction, when an obstruction occurs—such as one caused by snow or mud in the muzzle or by a shell of smaller gauge that lodges in front of the chamber—a bulge or burst can occur when the gun fires. In the extreme, a bulge can render the shotgun unusable; or the bulge can be slight and of no real consequence to the performance of the gun. In the early days of nontoxic steel shot, full-choked shotguns sometimes evidenced "ring bulge" at the choke constriction; this was visible, measuring about 0.005 to 0.010 inch. In fact, this bulge affected a single-barreled shotgun's performance but little. However, in double guns, ring bulge often caused the barrels to separate at the muzzle. See **barrel, barrel separation, burst barrel, nontoxic shot, steel shot**.

Bulino — A style of gun engraving that uses extremely fine strokes, resembling the engraving used to produce currency.

Bump (Brit.) — The portion of the butt of a shotgun stock just below the junction of the comb and butt. Often there is a pronounced bump at this point, and there can also be one at the toe. Carefully fitted, these provide for the contour of the shoulder and firmly anchor the stock into the shoulder pocket when the gun is mounted. See **comb, heel, toe**.

Bunker — See **Olympic trap**.

Burrard, Gerald — A British artillery officer in World War I, he is the author of a three-volume treatise entitled *The Modern Shotgun.*

Burst barrel — Anytime there is an obstruction in a shotgun barrel, it is possible and even probable that the barrel may burst upon firing. In double shotguns, the barrel normally fails in a longitudinal manner. In semiautomatic and pump-action shotguns, often the locking lugs will shear and much of the damage will be absorbed by the action, although both action and barrel may fail. There are few fatalities associated with burst barrels, although very often the explosion severely damages the shooter's hand or forearm nearest the point of the burst. In all cases, bursts are avoidable with a modicum of care. Under no circumstances clear an obstruction from the barrel by firing a shell; instead, use an appropriate cleaning rod or field-expedient cornstalk, tree branch, and so forth.

Butt — 1. See **buttstock**. 2. A blind or hide used in driven-game shooting to conceal the shooter from the flying grouse or partridge. Butts on some Scottish grouse moors are permanent structures resembling a shallow pit. Butts seen on driven partridge shoots in Spain are often holly bushes extended with additional cut branches placed to the sides. See **blind, hide**.

Butt: *Shooting driven red-legged partridge from a butt in Spain.*

Buttstock: *A collection of walnut buttstock blanks assembled by Griffin & Howe to allow their gunsmiths to select a superior blank for a restocking. Fine gunmakers worldwide have similar wood rooms.*

Butt marker — A set of small, numbered metal tags or other signs that identify the butts so that shooters know which butt is theirs, and to which butt to go when shooters rotate between drives. See **butt**.

Buttstock — The rearmost portion of a shotgun, which contacts the shoulder; the cheek is placed onto the buttstock during firing. The buttstock is perhaps the most important element of any shotgun, because if it properly fits the shooter, accuracy will be far better than if it does not. The shooter's eye is, in essence, the rear sight of the shotgun, and therefore the stock must consistently place the shooter's eye in precise alignment with the rib. In order for the fitter and the stocker to understand each other, a series of measurement points have become part of the nomenclature of the buttstock. These are the common descriptive terms: hand or grip—the area immediately behind the action, where the trigger hand grips the stock; comb—the top of the stock, where the shooter's cheek contacts the stock; butt—the extreme back of the stock, where it meets the shoulder; heel or bump—the rearmost top of the stock, where it meets the butt; toe—the lowest point on the butt; belly—the bottom portion of the stock. The following terms further define the buttstock, in terms of its dimensions: *Pull* is the measurement from the front trigger of a double-trigger gun, or from the single trigger to the center of the butt. *Drop at comb* defines the distance from the extended rib to the top of the front of the comb. *Drop at heel* is the measurement from the extended rib to the top of the heel. *Drop at face*, infrequently used, refers to a point about one-third to one-half the distance back from the point of the comb, where the shooter's face actually contacts the stock. *Cast off* is the bending of the stock to the right, as viewed from the rear and above, to accommodate a right-handed shooter's face. *Cast on* is the bending of the stock to the left to accommodate a left-handed shooter. Proper use of cast ensures that the comb is of the correct height, yet the configuration of the shooter's face is also accounted for by cast on or cast off. See **bend, cast off/ on, checkering, comb, drop, grip, hand, pull, recoil pad.**

Buttstock: *Ken Davies, Holland & Holland's senior shooting instructor, measuring a student's shotgun stock with a device that precisely determines the drop at comb and heel and cast off. These dimensions are the key to proper stock fit, which translates to the ability to predictably hit flying targets.*

Cacha (Sp.) — "Grip."

Caliber — The diameter of the bore of the gun or the diameter of the projectile, usually measured across the lands inside the bore and designated in either decimal fractions of English inches or in metric terms. Examples are 6.5mm or .260-caliber, 7mm or .280-caliber. The term is seldom used in reference to shotguns, except for the .410-bore and the rare 9.1mm cartridge.

Calico (Ital.) — "Butt of the stock."

Calls — Mouth- and hand-operated devices that reproduce the sounds made by waterfowl, crows, and varmints in order to lure them close enough to be shot. Of these, duck and goose calls are often works of art. Crows are called mainly by the use of electronic callers, although mouth-blown calls are equally effective. The calling of ducks and geese has become an area of great interest to hunters in the United States, and numerous custom call makers now turn out hundreds of handmade calls each year, in addition to the thousands of mass-produced calls sold by companies such as P. S. Olt and Haydel's.

Camera della cartucce (Ital.) — "Chamber."

Cane (Ital.) — "Hammer."

Canna (Ital.) — "Barrel."

Canon (Fr.) — "Barrel."

Cañon (Sp.) — "Barrel."

Canon rayé (Fr.) — Rifling in a shotgun barrel with a very slow twist to provide wide patterns.

Canting — During the mounting of a shotgun, a twisting of the shotgun toward or away from the face, causing the eye to be centered elsewhere than atop the rib. Canting is often referred to as cross-firing, because the eye is looking across the barrels rather than down them. See **rainbowing, rolling**.

Cap — See **percussion cap**.

Capsula (Ital.) — "Primer."

Càpsula fulminate (Sp.) — "Primer."

Cargador (Sp.) – "Magazine."

Caricatore (Ital.) — "Magazine."

Carmichel, Jim — Succeeding the late Jack O'Connor as shooting editor of *Outdoor Life,* Jim Carmichel has become one of the most influential gunwriters of all time. His monthly columns cover all phases of shooting, and his definitive reporting on all aspects of shotgunning have earned him the admiration and praise of the shooting public. Carmichel has an extensive test operation located near his northeastern Tennessee home, where he spends hours researching the latest in shooting technology. Known primarily for his excellent rifle marksmanship, Carmichel is a top-notch shotgunner.

Carrier — The part of the mechanism of a pump-action or semiautomatic shotgun onto which a fresh round from the magazine moves. On the forward cycle of the bolt, the carrier raises the new round up to the level of the chamber so that the breechbolt can push it in.

Cartouche (Fr.) — "Cartridge."

Cartridge — A self-contained round of ammunition. A cartridge consists of a case that contains the primer, propellant or powder, and projectiles. In the case of a shotshell, it is also necessary to have some type of wad. The wad seals the propellant gases, cushions the shot, and takes up sufficient room within the hull to ensure a proper, tight crimp. See **crimp, propellant, shot, wad.**

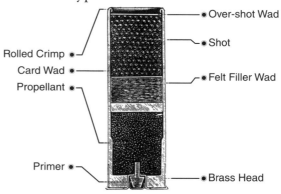

Rolled Crimp

Card Wad

Propellant

Primer

Over-shot Wad

Shot

Felt Filler Wad

Brass Head

Cartridge: *Two dummy rounds that have no live components, used to safely check the function of shotguns.*

Cartridge: *Shotshells, left to right: 3½-inch, 10-gauge; 3 ½-inch, 12-gauge; 3-inch, 12-gauge; 2¾-inch, 12-gauge field load; 2¾-inch, 12-gauge target load; 2¾-inch, 16-gauge; 3-inch, 20-gauge; 2¾-inch, 20-gauge; 2¾-inch, 24-gauge (obsolete); 2¾-inch, 28-gauge; 2-inch, 28-gauge; 2½-inch, 32-gauge (obsolete); 2½-inch, 36-gauge (obsolete); 2-inch, 36-gauge (obsolete); 3-inch, .410-bore; 2½-inch, .410-bore; and 2-inch, 9.1mm. (Not shown is the 2½-inch, 12-gauge.)*

Cartridge bag — A leather or canvas bag hunters use mostly for driven game shooting. Made in capacities to hold one hundred, two hundred, or more cartridges, these bags make reloading easy because of their large opening.

Cartridge bag

Cartridge magazine — A leather-covered wooden case used to transport large numbers of shotshells.

Cartuccia (Ital.) — "Cartridge."

Cartucho (Sp.) — "Cartridge."

Case — 1. The external portion of a cartridge, which holds all of the components. 2. A leather, canvas, or cloth cover shooters use for transporting a shotgun in an automobile or between butts or stations on a sporting clay course. 3. A hard, lockable case made of metal, wood, or plastic that affords maximum protection for a shotgun during transportation. See **oak and leather**.

Case hardening — A process whereby the surface of steel absorbs carbon and thereby is hardened, leaving the softer core free to flex. Traditional case hardening involves packing the steel parts in an iron box along with charcoal, animal bones, and leather. The case-hardening specialist then subjects the steel to a carefully controlled high temperature for a prescribed amount of time, followed by quenching of the parts in water. The result is an extremely hard surface—and a surface that is also beautiful, with colors running from blue to rich browns. Formulas for the packing of parts, optimum time, temperature, and quenching liquid vary. Far more common is the immersion of the parts in a vat of boiling cyanide, which also imparts color and hardens the surface. Cyanide hardening is far less costly, and the colors can be excellent; the hardness it produces, however, may not equal that of the charcoal method.

Case label — A leather or paper label, affixed by glue to the inside lid of a hard case, bearing the shotgun maker's name, address, and other information such as royal warrants, prizes, and so forth. Hard cases with such labels may add considerable value to shotguns.

Cased — 1. Legal terminology for a firearm transported in a case and thus inaccessible. 2. Gun-trade terminology designates a shotgun in some kind of case, often an oak-and-leather hard case supplied by the gun's original maker.

Cased with accessories — A term indicating that a shotgun has a hard or oak-and-leather case in which may be a variety of accessories, such as a jointed cleaning rod, bore brushes, a chamber brush, snap caps, extra strikers or firing pins, extra springs, an oil bottle, turnscrews, or a hand guard.

Cast off, cast on — The lateral bend put in a buttstock to compensate for the thickness of the shooter's face. Cast off is for right-handed shooters, cast on for those who are left-handed. In a bespoke or custom-stocked shotgun, cast is a part of the stock from the stock's head, where it meets the action, right through the butt. However, if there is no cast in the original stock, it is still possible to add it, either by removing some wood from the cheek side of the comb or by having the stock bent with heat and a bending jig. Stocks of proper height at the comb need cast to accommodate the structure of the shooter's face for the stock fit to be precise. Women shooters need additional cast at the toe of the stock to move it away from the breast.

Celtic engraving — A style of engraving that emphasizes strong, bold knots and strap work.

Centerfire — Ammunition in which the primer is in the center of the cartridge's head. See **primer, rimfire**.

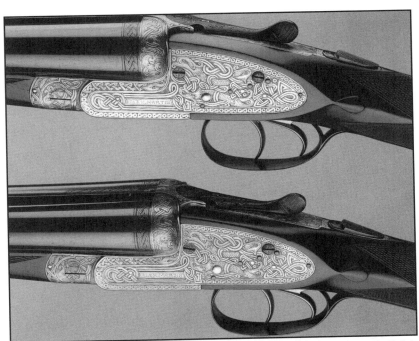

Celtic engraving: A pair of London-pattern sidelock ejectors with Celtic engraving by Alex Martin of Glasgow.

Chamber — The rearmost portion of the barrel, in which the cartridge rests prior to firing. Shotgun chambers vary in length and in diameter by gauge. There is a cut or rebate at the extreme rear of the chamber to accept the cartridge rim, and additional cuts at the rear of the chamber to accommodate the extractors. It is important that the ammunition be compatible with the chamber in which it will be fired. Firing an overly long cartridge in a chamber of shorter length results in abnormally high pressures, which may burst the barrel. Even if a burst does not occur, the fired hull will be difficult to extract, and the overly high pressures may eventually cause loosening of the action. See **barrel**.

Chamber: *A workman cutting the chambers in new over/under barrels.*

Chambre (Fr.) — "Chamber."

Chapuis Armes — Manufacturer located in Saint-Bonnet le Chateau, France, a maker of high-quality double rifles, over/unders, and side-by-sides.

Chargeur (Fr.) — "Magazine."

Checkering — A crosscut design that gunmakers cut into the grip or hand of the buttstock and fore-end; it is both decorative and functional. Well-executed checkering is beautiful to behold, and many custom shotguns display extensive and intricately checkered designs. Functionally, checkering provides a sure grip that guards against the hand's slipping under wet or cold conditions. In grading checkering, the higher the number of lines per inch, the finer the checkering. Traditionally, guns of low grade have checkering running eight to ten lines per inch. Better guns, such as the Grade One Winchester Model 21, have checkering from eighteen to twenty or twenty-two lines to the inch. High-grade checkering runs about twenty-seven or twenty-eight lines to the inch, although some checkering measures as high as thirty-two lines to the inch. However, extremely fine checkering, above twenty-six lines per inch, begins to feel smooth—defeating its function.

Checkering: *An example of finely executed checkering by Donny Gemes of Show-Me Gunstocks, Warsaw, Missouri, on a Model 21 fore-end.*

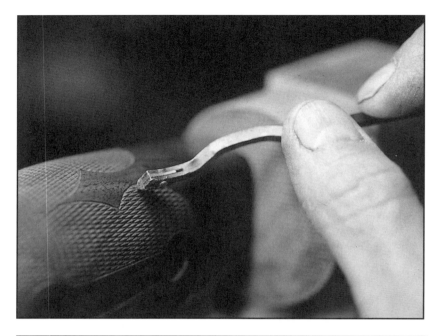

Checkering: *Custom gunsmith Greg Wolf finishing the checkering on a shotgun fore-end.*

Cheekpiece — Commonly found on shotguns of German make and combination guns, drillings, and vierlings, the cheekpiece is a projection of the stock on the face side of the stock. It is common on rifles, but there seems little need or use for one on a shotgun, save for a combination gun that will take a telescopic sight. Sometimes called a cheekrest.

Chequering (Brit.) — See **checkering**.

Chien (Fr.) — Lit. "dog," but also "hammer."

Choke — The interior constriction at the muzzle that shapes the shot charge. Degree of constriction runs from none, or cylinder, through extra full; gunmakers measure it in thousandths of an inch. American usage defines the various chokes as cylinder, skeet, improved cylinder, modified, improved modified, full, and extra full. The British often use the terms cylinder, quarter (improved cylinder), half (modified), three-quarter

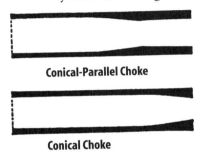

Conical-Parallel Choke

Conical Choke

(improved modified), and full. There are several types of choke that derive their names from the way in which they are cut into the barrel. Conical parallel choking indicates constriction by means of an elliptical radius leading to a parallel section, about an inch, of the desired constriction. Bespoke and other high-class shotguns are most likely to employ conical-parallel choking.

In swaged choking the exterior of the muzzle end of the barrel remains larger for an inch or two than the adjoining barrel. The gunmaker pulls the barrel through a cylindrical die that swages the extra material on the outside into a constriction in the inside. Only the cheapest of shotguns use this method of choking. Conical, or tapered, choking is the same as conical parallel, without the parallel section. A conical choke continues the conical or elliptical radius right to the muzzle. This type of choke is easy to create, by simply running the reamer into the barrel to varying depths, and some manufacturers use only one reamer, running it farther in for more open chokes.

Recessed, or jug, chokes are cut into the bore just behind the muzzle. This type of choking can restore choke to a shortened shotgun barrel. Gunmakers seldom use recessed chokes, owing to the ease of installing screw-in chokes.

Following are the specifications for common chokes in common gauges. Bear in mind that choke is a specific constriction measured against a specific bore. Each shotgun is different, and therefore the following are only generalizations:

Gauge	Diameter in inches	Choke	Constriction in inches
12	0.729	full	0.036
		improved modified	0.027
		modified	0.021
		improved cylinder	0.011
16	0.662	full	0.030
		improved modified	0.022
		modified	0.015
		improved cylinder	0.008
20	0.615	full	0.025
		improved modified	0.017
		modified	0.011
		improved cylinder	0.007
28	0.550	full	0.023
		improved modified	0.015
		modified	0.010
		improved cylinder	0.006
.410	0.410	full	0.020
		modified	0.010
		improved cylinder	0.005

Choke: *A barrel micrometer used to accurately measure the interior of shotgun barrels. The black ring is used to calibrate the micrometer before use.*

Choke: *Today's screw-in chokes provide the ultimate in versatility. On the left are extended chokes that place the constriction beyond the barrel; on the right are flush-mounted chokes that closely follow traditional bored chokes.*

Choke: *Here Becky Bowen is changing chokes prior to a round of sporting clays.*

Choke (Sp.) — "Choke."

Choke du canon (Fr.) — "Choke."

Choke gauge — A carefully machined device that gives an approximate idea of the choke constriction. To obtain a far more precise measurement of the choke, gunmakers use a barrel micrometer, which establishes both the cylinder bore of the barrel and the actual amount of constriction in comparison to barrel diameter.

Choke gauge: *A brass gauge by Galazan for checking the approximate amount of choke in a shotgun barrel.*

Choke, inventors of — In America, the first chokeboring of shotgun barrels was perhaps the work of an Illinois duck hunter named Fred Kimble, who claimed to have invented the choking of barrels in 1867. However, there is compelling proof that an American gunsmith, Sylvester Roper, who received his patent on 10 April 1866, was the true inventor of choke. W. R. Pape, of Newcastle, England, in parallel development also developed choked barrels in 1866, but Roper's patent preceded Pape's by about six weeks. W. W. Greener, in the first edition of *The Gun and Its Development*, dated 1881, credits the Spanish with choke; he credits the French in his ninth edition, and later credits himself with the first successful choke in 1874, following the receipt of a gun from Kimble. See **Roper, Kimble**.

Choke tubes — Interchangeable tubes or sleeves that screw into the muzzle of a shotgun barrel, varying the constriction and thereby influencing the pattern.

Choke tubes: *Three high-performance choke tubes pictured are: (Right to left) A threaded Briley full-choke turkey tube; Pattern Master, which uses raised projections, or "dogs," to catch and retard the wad; and the Terminator tube, which uses a series of gas ports linked by concentric channels to quickly bleed off high-pressure gases.*

Chopper lumps — Projection at the bottom of the breech end of the barrel on a side-by-side or single-barrel shotgun. Looking something like a chopping device, chopper lumps are an integral, forged part of the barrel. To create a side-by-side, the gunmaker joins the barrel normally by brazing or by dovetailing and pinning; the gunmaker then machines the lumps to accommodate the hinge pin and locking bolt. See **dovetail lumps, hinge pin, locking bolt, lumps.**

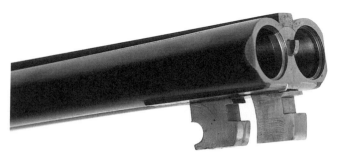

Chopper lumps: *The lumps on this AyA 53E are of the classic Purdey-style, engaging the double underbolt. Also visible is the Purdey-style concealed third fastener.*

Chrome-plated bores — Some gunmakers plate the inside of shotgun barrels with chromium for added rust and corrosion resistance and to provide a smoother surface against which the shot charge can slip.

Churchill, E. J. [Gunmakers] — High Wycombe, England. The continuation of the old-line London firm of gunmakers, best known for its one-time proprietor, Robert Churchill, author of the book *Game Shooting*. In it, Churchill outlined his now-famous method of shotgun shooting. See **Churchill, Robert.**

Churchill — A line of rather inexpensive semiautomatic, over/under, and side-by-side shotguns. Various companies import these guns. Not to be confused with shotguns made in England by E. J. Churchill.

Churchill rib — A narrow, high rib atop a side-by-side that tapers quickly from breech to muzzle. The gunmaker Robert Churchill devised this rib for use on his XXV (25-inch-barrel) shotguns so that, from the shooter's perspective, the barrels would appear to be longer.

Churchill, Robert — Robert Churchill (1886-1958), proprietor of

E. J. Churchill, a London best gunmaker, was controversial for his development, introduction, and dogmatic promotion of his XXV (25-inch-barrel) shotguns. His greatest and most lasting achievement, however, is the book he wrote with McDonald Hastings, entitled *Game Shooting*. In it, Churchill sets down his system of instinctive shooting, which has become the cornerstone of most contemporary shooting styles. Shooters worldwide use his method.

Churchill XXV — The shotgun developed by Robert Churchill that had 25-inch barrels topped with a high, tapered rib that gives the illusion that the barrels are longer. Introduced at a time when 28- and 30-inch barrels were in vogue, Churchill's shotgun engendered great criticism. Fast-handling and very precisely balanced, these guns have a following, yet the tapered rib flies in the face of Churchill's own shooting style, in which the shooters ignore the barrels, concentrating instead solely on the target.

Cilindrico (Ital.) — "Cylinder."

Cilindro (Sp.) — "Cylinder."

Circassian walnut — The traditional and legendary name for the finest gunstock wood, walnut from Circassia (Turkey).

Clay pigeon — See **clay target**.

Clay target — The universal name for a target made of a composition of pitch (tar) and clay that is hard enough to withstand handling by a mechanical throwing device yet brittle or soft enough that only a few shot pellets will break it. Clay targets come in a variety of colors, intended for contrast against various backgrounds. Popular colors are all-orange, all-white, and all-black, although some clubs prefer that only the dome portion be painted. The standard clay target for trap, skeet, and many sporting clay stations measures $1\frac{1}{8}$ inches in height and is $4\frac{1}{4}$ inches in diameter. The midi is $3\frac{1}{2}$ inches in diameter and 1 inch thick. The mini target is $2\frac{1}{4}$ inches in diameter and $\frac{7}{8}$ inch thick. The battue is a very thin $4\frac{1}{4}$-inch target of extremely hard composition that makes possible highly erratic flight. The rabbit is a standard $4\frac{1}{4}$-inch-dimension target of hard composition that is bounced along the ground.

Cleaning game — For feathered game, first remove the feathers by either plucking or skinning. Then remove the wings, followed by the intestines. To eviscerate a bird, make a cut with a sharp knife through the soft tissue at the rear bottom of the bird. Remove the entrails by inserting the

Clay target: *Informal clay-target shooting with a manually operated trap and a safe backstop is a good way to keep in shape for field shooting.*

hand—or, in the case of small birds like bobwhite quail, the fingers—into the body cavity and pulling them out. Take care also to remove the lung tissue that runs along the backbone. In some cases, such as mourning doves and geese, keep only the breast meat. In the case of doves, slit the skin over the breastbone and pull it back, then insert a finger under the back of the breastbone and pull the breast from the carcass. You may want to smoke goose, or cook the bird over a charcoal or gas grill, much like a beefsteak. Remove the skin and then use a sharp knife to detach the meat from the breastbone.

Cleaning kit — The collection of items necessary to clean a shotgun. Various kits are available, from the most basic and utilitarian through the wooden-cased variety with rods made of exotic woods. The items you will need are a rod of sufficient length to pass through the barrels, a set of tips for pushing and pulling cloth patches through the bore, a bronze bore brush, and a chamber brush. In addition, you must have a bottle of solvent to dissolve plastic and powder residue and a bottle of lubricant.

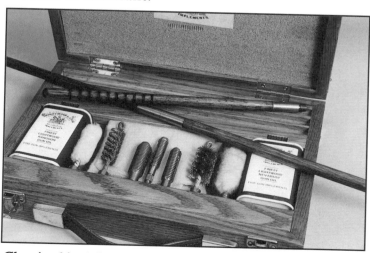

Cleaning kit: A full-service cleaning kit that includes a rod, various brushes and jags to hold the cleaning patches, bore cleaner, and lubricating oil.

Tip the rod—preferably one of wood or aluminum, so as not to scratch the bore—with a loop and a patch that fits the bore (but is not too tight). Saturate the patch with solvent and pass it through the barrel several times, uniformly wetting the bore. It is then best to wait several minutes so that the solvent has time to work. Then dip the bore brush into the solvent and pass it through the bore five or ten times, making sure that the brush exits the bore on both ends so that the bristles are not bent only in one direction. Following this brushing, insert the chamber brush into the chamber and rotate, scrubbing the chamber clean. Again allow the barrel to sit for a few minutes; then, finally, remove all residue by pushing a series of tight-fitting patches through the barrel. Repeat until the patches come out clean and no streaks of lead or plastic are visible. Following cleaning of the bore, wipe all traces of solvent from adjoining exterior surfaces, then apply a lubricant to the bearing surfaces. In the case of a double gun, apply grease to the hinge pin, hook, action bar knuckle, and mating surface of the fore-end. Use a tiny drop of oil on the moving parts of repeaters, but the rule is to use only minute amounts: Excess lubrication flows back into the action and thence into the head of the buttstock, often doing severe damage by softening the wood.

Cocking dogs — See **cocking levers**.

Cocking indicators — A throwback to the transition from hammer to hammerless shotguns, cocking indicators are projections on the top or side of the action of a double gun that, when protruding, indicate that the tumblers or hammers are cocked and the piece is ready to fire. Cocking indicators can also be plain or gold-filled cuts on the hammer pin of a sidelock gun that indicate whether the hammer is cocked by the position of the cut.

Cocking levers — Levers that usually project through the bar or knuckle of the action and engage the fore-end iron at one end and the tumblers at the other. When the fore-end iron rotates downward, the levers bear against the tumblers, rotating them sufficiently for the sears to engage the sear notch. See **action bar, notch, sear**.

Cocking limb — See **cocking levers**.

Cocking spring — See **sear spring**.

Color case hardening — Term directed at the aesthetics of case hardening rather than the surface hardness imparted to the metal. In use one follows the other.

Colombarie (Sp.) — A form of live pigeon shooting in Mexico and Texas. Rather than releasing pigeons from a trap, a thrower, or *colombarie*, stands directly in front of the shooter and on the shooter's command throws the bird. The *colombarie* often pulls feathers from the wings or tail of a bird, making it fly erratically. As in other pigeon shooting, betting on both the *colombarie* and/ or shooter is common. See **box birds, pigeon shooting**.

Comb — The topmost part of the buttstock, against which the shooter's face rests. See **buttstock, cheekpiece, drop, Monte Carlo**.

Combination gun — A shoulder-fired firearm that combines rifled and smooth-bored barrels. The most common combination gun is the drilling, which normally incorporates two shotgun barrels with a rifled barrel, most often firing a centerfire cartridge. Other configurations can combine two rifled barrels with a single shotgun barrel; the combinations are infinite. See **centerfire, drilling, vierling**.

Commission Internationale Permanente — Also called the International Proof Commission (C.I.P.), this organization was formed in 1914 to standardize proof, pressure measurement, chamber and bore size, and cartridge dimensions. As of 1993, the following countries were members: Austria, Belgium, Chile, Czechoslovakia, Finland, France, Germany, Hungary, Italy, Spain, and the United Kingdom.

Company terms (Brit.) — Terms coined to describe various groups of birds or animals: a nye of pheasants, a paddling of ducks, a fall of woodcock, a skulk of foxes, a cete of badgers, a singular of boars, a pride of lions, a siege of herons, a herd of swans, a spring of teal, a covert of coots, a gaggle of geese (a flock on the water), a skein of geese (a flock in flight), a sord of mallards, a company of wigeon, a trip of waterfowl, a dopping of sheldrakes (mergansers), a bevy of quail, a covey of partridge or grouse, a pack of grouse (more than one covey), a walk of snipe (on the ground or water), a wisp of snipe (in flight), a murmuration of starlings, a cast of hawks, a sleuth of bears, a gang of elk. All largely unused, the terms are great fun.

Composed pair – A pair of shotguns, normally side-by-sides but also over/unders, that are alike in stock dimensions, barrel length, weight, and balance, but not made as a pair. Composed pairs are most frequently by the same maker, but in other instances, two separate guns not by the same maker but quite similar in weight, balance, and feel have been paired. Although not a matched or true pair, and certainly not of the value of either a matched or true pair, a composed pair can still serve a shooter very well in the field. See **matched pair, true pair.**

Composite pair — See **composed pair.**

Concave rib — A rib that is dished or concave throughout its length so that the shooter looks down a shallow "U" rather than the more common flat matte or ventilated rib. See **hollow rib, matte rib, rib, ventilated rib.**

Condition — An arbitrary rating of a firearm for the purpose of valuation. The National Rifle Association of America, the *Blue Book of Gun Values*, and auction houses all use various grading methods for assigning condition.

C

Connecticut Shotgun Manufacturing Company — Founded by Antony Galazan. In mid-1992 he obtained the rights from Savage Arms to resume manufacture of A. H. Fox shotguns in a modern plant in New Britain, Connecticut. Galazan produces only higher-grade Fox shotguns, perhaps the finest American-made shotgun manufactured today. The company also produces the A. Galazan Over-and-Under, and tools and accessories for the gun industry.

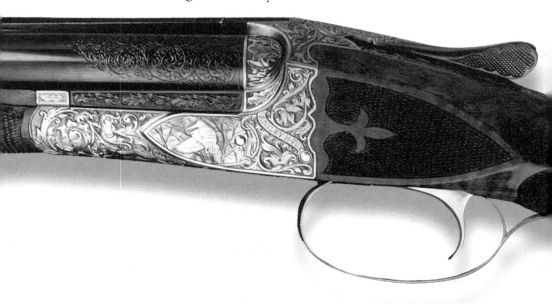

Connecticut Shotgun Manufacturing Company: *The Connecticut Shotgun Manufacturing Company, under Antony Galazan, is at the forefront of fine gunmaking and has led the renaissance in fine American shotgun manufacturing over the past ten years. Shown here is one of their recent A. H. Fox guns.*

Connecticut Valley Classics — Currently (as of 1999) manufactured by Cooper Arms, Stevensville, Montana. For all intents and purposes, these are reproductions of the Winchester 101 over/under that was made in Japan for Olin/Winchester and later Classic Doubles. In 1987 the factory in Tochigi City, Japan, ceased production of the Olin/Winchester Classic Doubles 101; Connecticut Valley Classics then began production of this popular over/under.

Conversion — In early shotguns and firearms, the term "conversion" generally indicates modernization to a more efficient ignition system—that is, flint to percussion, or pinfire to centerfire. The term can also mean conversion of a shotgun from a larger to a smaller gauge. During the 1960s, gunsmith Claude Purbaugh and Simmons Gun Specialties converted 20-gauge Remington 1100 semiautomatics to 28-gauge and .410-bore for skeet shooting.

Cosmi, Americo & Figlio — The Cosmi semiautomatic shotgun is unique in that the magazine is under the action and extends back into the buttstock; the action breaks open like a double gun, exposing the chamber and magazine for loading. Established in Torrette, Italy, in 1930, Cosmi has produced approximately 7,000 of these unique shotguns.

Crab joint — 1. A joint peculiar to Westley Richards shotguns, named for its similarity to the joints of crab. 2. A tongue of wood that covers the hinge or joint of the barrels and action.

Crescent Fire Arms Company, Norwich, Connecticut — A producer of shotguns from 1888 to 1893. In the 1900s it merged with N. R. Davis and H.&D. Folsom to form Crescent-Davis. Crescent made shotguns for many companies. See **Folsom, H&D.**

Crimp — The part of a shotshell that closes over the shot, preventing its spilling, and that provides a stiff end to the shell to ensure smooth chambering. Over the centuries, crimps have taken essentially two forms, the rolled and folded or the pie-style crimp, named for its resemblance to a freshly sliced pie. Rolled crimps relied on a stiff over-shot wad to retain the shot; the edges were tightly rolled down to hold the wad. Upon firing, the wad frequently disturbed the pattern. The pie-style crimp uses a 6- or 8-segment fold of the end of the shell, effectively sealing it. Early brass shotshells also used over-the-shot wads, the end of the brass shell being slightly crimped or the wad glued into place.

The importance of the crimp, beyond appearance and feeding, is that upon firing, the crimp must retard the forward movement of the wad and shot column until the primer has properly ignited the propellant. Reloads that have a weak crimp often fail to provide expected velocities, and most often manifest themselves in flames exiting the muzzle, flames in the ejection port, or flames coming from the joint of the breech and barrels. While not dangerous, such flaming is a sure indication of poor crimps. The propellant is only partially ignited, and rather than burning efficiently within the hull and providing proper velocity, it burns so poorly that it is not completely consumed within the barrel.

*Crimp: Three styles of crimp. (**Left to right**) Rolled crimp; folded crimp; heat-sealed folded crimp.*

Crosse (Fr.) — "Butt."

Crossbolt — A method of locking a shotgun closed for firing. Most commonly the crossbolt engages an extension from between the barrels that mates into a corresponding groove in the face of the action. Using a carefully matched opening of the precise diameter of the crossbolt pin, the extension and pin tightly lock the breech down during firing. Crossbolts commonly couple with a Purdey underbolt as an additional and often unnecessary locking device. See **action, face, underbolt**.

Crossbolt: *Crossbolts are either round or rectangular. This drilling has a round crossbolt.*

Cross-eyed stock — Also called a cross-over stock, the cross-eyed stock is a buttstock made with an extreme amount of cast on or cast off so that the shooter shoulders the gun on one side of the body but sights using the eye on the opposite side. For example, a shooter mounts the shotgun on his right shoulder but uses his left eye. This style of stock will also accommodate a person who is severely cross-eyed, although it is often recommended that rather than use this style of stock, the shooter learn to shoot from the shoulder on the side of the good eye.

Cross pin — See **hinge pin**.

Crow hunting/shooting — Crows can provide off-season practice. Crow hunters normally use decoys and electrically operated callers. It is important to hide well, as crows are very wary and possess good eyesight.

Cube shot — Shot cast in the form of a cube, making it extremely unstable ballistically and causing the resulting pattern to be very wide. Cube shot is a form of spreader shot that enables the shotgunner shooting a tightly choked shotgun to have more than normally open patterns. Used only in Europe, cube shot is the equivalent of the American brush load, which makes use of various wads to spread the shot pattern.

Culata (Sp.) — "Butt."

Culata delantera (Sp.) — "Fore-end."

Cutoff — In semiautomatic shotguns, the cutoff holds the shells in the magazine while the chamber is emptied. See **magazine cutoff.**

Cutts Compensator — A device whose original function was to reduce the muzzle climb of the Browning Automatic Rifle and Thompson submachine gun. Its inventor was Col. Richard M. Cutts, U.S. Marine Corps, Ret. The rights to the Cutts Compensator became the property of the Lyman Gunsight Company in 1929, and they adapted it for use on pump and semiautomatic shotguns. In use, the vented vanes direct the propellant gases slightly back toward the breech of the shotgun. This helps reduce recoil. In addition, the Cutts Compensator uses interchangeable choke tubes that are screwed into the front of the device. The Cutts Compensator has all but disappeared on hunting shotguns, although some skeet competitors still use it.

Cylindre (Fr.) — "Cylinder."

D

Dakota Arms, Inc. — Sturgis, South Dakota. One of the many current importers of side-by-side shotguns in the United States. Of Italian manufacture, these are high-quality game guns.

Dakota Arms, Inc: *Dakota Arms started making their own round-action shotguns in the 1990s. Depicted here is a 20-gauge limited edition Legend grade, which is top of the line. These guns can be made in any gauge and come in an oak and leather case.*

Damascus barrel — Gunmakers produced Damascus barrels by twisting strands of steel and iron together, then winding them around a mandrel. Because of the alternating pattern such

Gun-barrel iron, twisted, and laid into a riband.

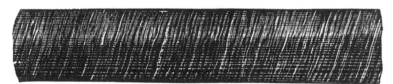

Two-iron Damascus barrel.

Skelp gun-barrel.

Three-iron stub Damascus barrel.

Single-iron Damascus barrel.

ribbons of steel and iron produce, these barrels are often exquisitely beautiful, a beauty enhanced by acid etching. The finest-quality Damascus barrels can—if properly cared for and properly proof tested—be capable of firing smokeless powder. However, Damascus barrels of less than first quality, or those allowed to corrode and pit, can deteriorate to the point of being unsafe with any ammunition. Exercise extreme care if you wish to fire a Damascus-barrel shotgun. Have a competent gunsmith inspect the gun, and submit it for re-proof if there is any question. See **proofing, twist barrel**.

Darne — A French gunmaker who made side-by-side shotguns using a unique sliding breech system. Rather than breaking open, the breech of the Darne slides open rearward, in line with the barrels. The shooter rolls the gun to one side or the other, and the spent and extracted hulls drop off. A lever opens and closes the action—forward to open, backward to close. Paul Bruchet continues to manufacture this sleek shotgun of unique design under the Darne name. See **Bruchet, Paul**.

Data manual — A book or booklet containing formulas for the loading of cartridges. Anyone undertaking the handloading of ammunition should invest in a data manual, then precisely follow the recommendations to produce both safe and ballistically balanced loads. Deviation from listed data can result in loads with dangerously high pressures and often of substandard performance.

Davies, Ken — Chief instructor at the Holland & Holland shooting grounds. The subject of several videotapes on shooting, Davies (pronounced "Davis") is also the author of *The Better Shot*, a print version of the shooting instruction provided by Holland & Holland.

Deckplatte (Ger.) — "Side plate."

Decoys — Wooden, cork, or plastic models of waterfowl, pigeons, mourning doves, crows, and other birds, used to lure them to the gun. Decoys were originally carved from wood, and wooden decoys are now considered highly collectible, often selling for tens of thousands of dollars at decoy auctions and private sales.

Hunters arrange plastic decoys of ducks and geese to look like resting, feeding birds in order to entice other waterfowl to

Decoys: *A variety of duck and goose decoys used in hunting waterfowl.*

join them. Crows respond to decoys set to resemble a flock engaged in combat with an owl or a hawk; therefore, owls are frequently added to crow decoy spreads. Doves are attracted to other birds in a feeding field, and hunters often place plastic dove decoys on fences or in trees. Pigeons, like waterfowl, will land in a spread of decoys, and in Great Britain and South America hunters rig decoys for pigeon shooting.

de Grey, Earl — See **Ripon, Lord**.

Demi-bloc — See **monobloc**.

Dents — The steel of shotgun barrels is relatively soft and thin. Consequently, denting is not uncommon. If a dent occurs, have it raised before firing the gun again. Shooting a shotgun with a dent may cause the dented area to substantially wear, which will decrease the barrel thickness at that point. A qualified gunsmith can raise all but the most severe dents and if necessary restrike the barrels and blue or blacken them—removing all but the memory of the damage. A severely dented barrel may require sleeving, or in the case of a pump or semiautomatic, the purchase of a new barrel. See **sleeved barrels**.

Detachable locks — A type of removable lock most common to sidelock double guns. Detachable locks are not, however, restricted to sidelocks; Westley Richards offers a droplock on their over/under and side-by-sides, and the German Blitz action is common to shotguns such as the Italian-made Perazzi. The advantages of detachable locks are ease of cleaning and lubrication, ease of repair, and, in the case of malfunction or damage, the possibility of field replacement. See **Blitz action, sidelock**.

Détente (Fr.) — "Trigger."

Detonating (Brit.) — A term used by the British for the standing breech of a double gun. See **standing breech**.

Detonators (Brit.) — See **fences**.

Diamond hand — Style of straight grip or hand in which a cross-section resembles a diamond with a slight peak at top and bottom and both sides. This type of grip is very pleasing in the hand. See **grip hand**.

Dickson, John & Son — Scottish gunmakers in Edinburgh since 1840. The last of the Dickson family left the business in 1923. Most famous for the Dickson round action side-by-side. See **Dickson round action, round action**.

Dickson round action — A stylish side-by-side action that is rounded on the bottom. The true greatness of this action lies in the fact that it is a trigger-plate action that carries the locks on the trigger plate. With no working parts in the action, it is immensely strong and can be made quite small. Coupled with the rounded bar, the Dickson round action is, in the eyes of many, the equal of any sidelock in function and beauty.

Dipped finish – A proprietary camouflage finish applied by dipping a prepared shotgun into a bath on which floats a membrane carrying the camouflage or wood-grain finish. The membrane tightly adheres to the gun, providing a permanent finish in various camouflage patterns.

Disconnector — The device, normally a lever, in the action of a pump or semiautomatic shotgun that disconnects the trigger from the sear during the cycling of the gun.

Without a disconnector, the shotgun would fire the instant the breechbolt is locked if the trigger were held rearward. In a semiautomatic, that would amount to its being a machine gun. The Winchester Model 12 pump did not have a disconnector and therefore could be fired the instant the slide locked the bolt into battery.

Disk-set strikers — Strikers or firing pins held into the face of the action by a bushing. By means of a special wrench, it is possible to replace a broken firing pin quickly in the field. Should the firing pin opening or hole erode owing to leaking gas, a gunsmith can replace the entire bushing.

Disk set strikers: This AyA 53E action shows the two bushings through which the shooter can quickly remove the firing pins, should one break. Also evident are the side clips that prevent sideways motion and the concealed third fastener.

Dispersante (Fr.) — A shell loaded for or by Fabrique Nationale in which the shot is in the form of cubes rather than spheres. The intent was that the aerodynamically inefficient cubes would very quickly spread, providing an open pattern from a tightly choked barrel. See **plomb disco, spreader wad**.

Dog pin — A pin around which the cocking lever or dog rotates upon opening the action of a single-barrel, side-by-side, or over/under. See **cocking dog, cocking levers**.

Doll's head — A rearward projection of the rib of a double-barrel shotgun that mates into a similarly shaped cut on the top of the action. So named because of the round top that resembles the neck and head of a child's doll. Some saw the doll's head as adding strength to the action of a shotgun; in truth, unless the fit is very precise, they serve little purpose. Although Westley Richards originated 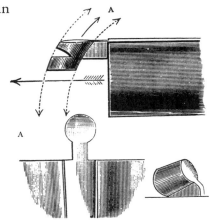 the doll's head, they are most common on Parker shotguns.

Doppelflinten (Ger.) — "Double-barrel shotgun."

Double Automatic — Developed by Val Browning, son of John Moses Browning, and listed in the Browning catalog from 1952 through 1971, the Browning Double Automatic was a short-recoil operated shotgun that carried one shell in the chamber and another in a cutout in the receiver. A lightweight gun that cycled extremely fast, it became popular with Southern quail hunters, especially in the Twelvette model that had its receiver machined from aluminum, making it a very light shotgun and one that was ahead of its time. The major drawback to this shotgun was that it was very butt-heavy and muzzle-light, making it feel unbalanced in the hands.

Double-barrel — A shotgun having two barrels placed either side-by-side or one atop the other as an over/under.

Double triggers — Found on side-by-side and over/under shotguns and double rifles. Each barrel has its own independent locks and trigger. In normal use, the front trigger fires the right barrel of a side-by-side and the bottom barrel of an over/under, the rear or back trigger firing the remaining barrel. In use, double triggers have the advantage of the instant selection of choke without the manipulation of a barrel selector, and, should a lock fail to fire, the instant availability of a second shot. See **articulated trigger, barrel selector, single trigger**.

Doubles at all stations — A form of American-style skeet in which the shooter tries to break two simultaneously thrown targets with the two shots allowed. The shooter takes the high-house target first from stations one through four; from positions five through seven the shooter takes the low-house target first. The pattern is the same on the return with the exception of station four, from which the shooter takes the low target first. Breaking both targets with the same shot means that only the first target counts as dead, and the trapper releases a fresh pair to establish the second bird. During this proof sequence, the shooter must fire at the first bird in order for the second shot to count. This form of skeet often serves as a tie-breaker in tournaments following the shooting of one hundred or two hundred conventional targets, and it is often a separate event at larger competitions.

Doubling — The simultaneous firing of both barrels of a double shotgun. Doubling normally results from a misadjusted trigger or other problem with the trigger, sear, or sear engagement. Employ the services of a competent gunsmith to correct doubling.

Dovetailed lumps – 1. A method of attaching lumps to round bar barrels by machining a dovetail slot between the barrels (which have been machined flat to fit together) and fitting in a set of lumps. The whole is then brazed. 2. Patented in 1911 by G. Norman, a gun designer at Birmingham Small Arms (B.S.A.), this is a system whereby the two chopper lumps of the two barrels of a side-by-side join by means other than the traditional welding or brazing. In this method, perhaps best used in the Winchester Model 21, one lump has a male dovetail and the other a female. A pin or screw secures the two lumps together. The result is an extremely sturdy lump that avoids the need to apply high heat to the lumps and barrels to weld or braze them, and the consequent possibility of warping.

Down-the-line — A form of trapshooting competition in which the competitors shoot twenty-five targets on each of four different trap fields. In this sequence, the squad shoots twenty-five targets, then moves to the adjoining trap and shoots twenty-five more, until completing the prescribed number of targets—normally one hundred.

Drilling (Ger.) — A combination gun with three barrels. The term derives from the German *drei*, for "three," meaning three-barreled. See **combination gun**.

Drilling: *Drillings are amazingly versatile. This hunter shot a coyote with a 12x12 gauge with a .30-06 barrel below. With a quick-detachable scope mount and a full-length .22 Hornet insert in the right 12-gauge barrel, this gun is set up to shoot anything from a quail to an elk—even a ground squirrel.*

Driven game shooting — As practiced primarily in Great Britain, Spain, and other parts of Europe, the shooters wait in small butts or blinds and a number of beaters slowly drive the birds—red-legged partridge, red grouse, or pheasant—toward the line of guns. British driven shooting blossomed with the development of the breechloading shotgun, and it reached its zenith in the years immediately prior to World War I. Driven shooting is not only a sport but also a social event. Many spent fortunes keeping up with the driven game circle, which included kings and other royalty. Today, driven shooting is very costly, but it has a good following. In Britain the pheasant is the prime driven bird; in Spain it is the red-legged partridge, and Scotland features the red grouse.

Driven game shooting: *The loader on the right and a pick-up boy carefully mark the shooter's downed birds on a driven partridge shoot in Spain.*

Driven game shooting: *The beaters nearing the line of guns.*

Driven game shooting: *Shooting at a driven red-legged partridge in Spain.*

Drop — The measurement taken at the topmost surface of a shotgun's stock that determines the elevation of the shooter's head and eye in relation to the bore of the barrel. In measuring drop, the gunmaker lays a straightedge upon the rib or top of the barrels and measures from the bottom of the straightedge to the top of the stock. See **buttstock, drop at comb, drop at face, drop at heel**.

Drop at comb — One of the essential measurements for fitting a shotgun stock. The gunmaker measures drop at comb at the very front top of the comb.

Drop at face — An optional measurement of drop that the gunfitter may take midway between the front, top surface of the comb and the heel. It is the point at which the shooter's face contacts the stock. Because of the variation in exact placement, drop at face is often not a major factor in gun fitting.

Drop at heel — A vital measurement in determining the placement of the shooter's head and eye on the gunstock. Drop at heel is a measurement the gunfitter takes at the farthest end of the buttstock, where the buttplate or recoil pad meets the top of the comb.

Drop lock — A lock designed and patented by John Deeley and Leslie Taylor in 1897, and used on shotguns manufactured by Westley Richards. Encased in a boxlock-style action, the locks, each of which contains the hammer or tumbler, mainspring, and sear, fit into two slim recesses on either side of the action. A hinged plate on the bottom of the action holds them in place. To remove them, open this bottom plate and the locks drop into the hand, hence their name.

Drop points — A transitional decorative motif on the sides of the stock of a double shotgun just behind the action and before the area of the grip. The use of drop points goes back to early flintlocks, in which, as with contemporary shotguns, they make a pleasing optical transition from the action to the stock but serve no other purpose.

Dropped shot — A term that defines shot made with only 0.5 percent antimony. In the early years of the twentieth century, many felt this shot to be superior for hunting quail, believing that it flattened upon impact, making it more lethal. The fact is that because so much of the soft shot deformed upon firing, the resulting pattern was very large; hence on close-flushing quail many birds found their way into the bag that would have escaped a tighter pattern.

Duck load — A term hunters use to describe a heavy load for shooting wild ducks. Because there are many ways to hunt ducks, there is no single duck load. In areas where hunters may still use lead shot, and in terms of traditional selections, Nos. 4, 5, or 6 lead are historically the choice of hunters for most ducks.

Further complicating matters is the current requirement in the United States and elsewhere that hunters use nontoxic shot for duck. Some general rules apply: Over decoys at ranges of less than thirty-five yards, No. 3 steel is acceptable. For ducks beyond thirty-five and out to a maximum of fifty yards, No. 2 steel is appropriate. Shoot small ducks such as teal with smaller-size steel shot of No. 3, 4, or even No. 6, if they are within twenty-five yards. Alternative nontoxic pellets such as bismuth provide more conventional selections: No. 4 for decoying ducks, No. 2 for passing shots. Tungsten-polymer, because it can equal the density of lead shot, provides the most traditional selection of sizes, with Nos. 3, 4, 5, or 6 appropriate for even large ducks like mallards.

Shell length is often a consideration, and some hunters use the three-inch magnum. However, in terms of payload, a 2¾-inch, 12-gauge shell loaded with 1¼ ounces of lead has, historically, accounted for the most ducks bagged. When dealing with nontoxic shot, the 12-gauge load of 1¼ to 1³/₈ ounces of steel, or a similar load of bismuth or tungsten-polymer, is an excellent choice. One should keep in mind that there are favorite regional loads that incorporate local experience; if they fit the general criteria outlined above, they should be an acceptable choice.

Ducks Unlimited — The first of several conservation organizations in the United States that raise money for the acquisition of habitat and the study of waterfowl, with the goal of producing stable, enduring, and huntable populations of ducks and geese.

Ducks Unlimited: *National Headquarters in Memphis, Tennessee.*

Dynamit Nobel RWS, Inc. — U.S. importer of Brenneke slugs and shotgun ammunition and Rottweil shotguns. See **Rottweil**.

Ear plugs — See **hearing protection.**

Eccentric choke — A bored, fixed choke or specially fitted choke tube that causes the shot charge to be directed in a specific direction. In certain applications, some trapshooters prefer to have their pattern thrown an exact number of inches above center. That is possible through the use of a carefully regulated eccentric choke. In other applications, a poorly regulated double gun can be made to shoot to point of impact through the use of eccentric choking.

Eibar, Spain — The historical center of the Spanish shotgun-making region. Located in the heart of the Basque region in northern Spain, it is home to virtually all of the Spanish shotgun trade.

Éjecteur (Fr.) — "Ejector."

Ejection port — An elliptical aperture on the upper side of the action of a semiautomatic or pump-style shotgun that provides an opening through which the fired shotshell ejects during the first part of the cycling of the gun's action. On some pump-action shotguns the ejection port is on the bottom.

Ejector — The part of a breechloading shotgun that throws the spent or fired hull free of the gun. In most double shotguns, ejectors operate by means of springs and hammers or tumblers located in the fore-end. Upon firing, the sear that holds the ejector hammer comes free so that the hammer can move forward with sufficient force to hit the bottom of the extractor, propelling the fired shell from the chamber. In the case of an unfired shell, the ejector-hammer sear does not free the hammer, and the extractor simply lifts the unfired shell clear of the chamber. On pump and semiautomatic shotguns the ejector is normally a stud or other projection at the

Ejector: *A workman fitting the ejectors to a pair of barrels.*

rear of the barrel extension or receiver, on the side opposite the ejection port. The extractor holds the fired shell to the breechbolt face until it tips sideways from the gun as a result of hitting the ejector and flies out through the ejection port. Many individuals confuse the extractor with the ejector, especially on repeating shotguns. See **extractor, nonejector**.

Eley — One of the largest shotshell manufacturing companies in Great Britain.

Eley: The British company Eley still makes shells with a paper hull.

Engraving — A design cut into the metal of a firearm. In its most basic form, engraving can mean the simple cutting of the manufacturer's name onto the barrels or action, along with various patent numbers that cover the design of the gun and the caliber, gauge, and chamber length. More elaborate engraving may include artistic renderings of dogs, game birds, animals, nude women—images limited only by the imagination and skill of the engraver. See **bulino, Celtic engraving, rose and scroll**.

Engraving: *An engraver working on a side-by-side action.*

Escopetas de dos cañones (Sp.) — "Double-barrel shotgun."

Espulsore (Ital.) — "Ejector."

Estate — The British equivalent of a farm that raises game birds, normally pheasants, for the purpose of selling them to guests who shoot them as driven game. This sale of birds provides added income to the estate or farm.

Estate Cartridge — An American ammunition company in Texas that specializes in loading proprietary ammunition.

Estate Cartridge: *Estate Cartridge Company of Conroe, Texas, makes 2½-inch shells especially for the American shooter.*

Estrattore (Ital.) — "Extractor."

Etiquette (Brit.)—The rules by which one shoots game. Etiquette deals mainly with rules of safety, but it can also extend to dress, style of shotgun used, and so forth. Although a somewhat formal term, etiquette is really the manner in which shooting takes place, and it bears mainly upon the safe deportment of the shooters. Those who breach shooting etiquette may not receive an invitation to return, being branded as unsafe shooters. See **Walsingham, Lord**.

Expulsor (Sp.) – "Ejector."

Extracteur (Fr.) — "Extractor."

Extractor — The part of the action that extracts the shotshell

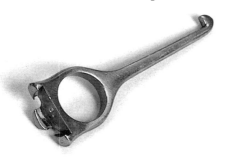

from the chamber. Some— normally inexpensive— single, over/under, and double shotguns use only extractors, requiring the shooter to remove the fired shells manually. In pump and semiautomatic repeaters the extractor, normally a spring-loaded hook on the side of the breechbolt toward the ejection port, pulls the fired hull from the chamber after firing and holds it to the face of the bolt until the ejector throws it free. See **ejector.**

Extractor: A manual extractor of the type that proved very useful during the age of paper-cased shotshells but that was rendered largely redundant by the universal use of plastic hulls, which do not swell in wet weather.

Extractor (Sp.) — "Extractor."

Eye dominance — Since one does not sight a shotgun like a rifle but rather points it, it is important that the shooter's eye that is in line with the barrel be the shooter's dominant eye. Although some individuals have central vision, where both eyes are of equal strength, most people have one eye that is dominant. Commonly it is the eye that corresponds with the hand the person uses for writing. However, it is not uncommon—and relatively more common among women than men—for the dominant eye to be on the opposite side: that is, a right-handed person with a left dominant eye.

To determine eye dominance one need only point at an object across a room with both eyes open. Then alternately close first one eye, then the other, the pointing finger will either remain pointing at the object or jump away. If for example a person is right-handed and points at an object with the right forefinger, then closes the left eye, the person can be said to be right-eye dominant if the finger remains aligned. However, if upon closing the left eye the finger jumps away, that person is left-eye dominant.

A shotgunner who is left-eye dominant and who shoots from the right shoulder, or vice versa, will find it difficult to hit moving targets consistently. The solution may be to squint or close the dominant eye, to place a piece of opaque tape over the lens of the shotgunner's shooting glasses on the dominant side, or, more radically, to learn to shoot from the side of the dominant eye. Those with central vision will also find one of these solutions helpful. In any case, if you suspect that your dominant eye is opposite your shooting side, seek the advice of an instructor.

Eye protection — In any shooting sport the eyes are vulnerable to damage. Ricocheting pellets, unburned propellant or powder, wind-driven pellet buffer, a separated case, a burst barrel, and other dangers lurk on both shooting range and in the field. Most ranges will deny admission to anyone not equipped with some kind of eye protection. In upland hunting in close cover, eyeglasses are a must to keep branches from hitting the eyes, and even when waterfowl hunting, wind-driven buffer is a problem.

For those who routinely wear eyeglasses, an optometrist can make a set that rides high on the face and has hardened lenses. Those who wear contact lenses or who do not need corrective lenses can purchase special shooting glasses at very reasonable cost with an assortment of colored lenses to meet just about any light or background condition. Those wearing prescription glasses can also order prescription-ground shooting glasses that offer both good vision and protection. It is imperative that all shooters recognize the need for eye protection and wear protective glasses whenever shooting a firearm.

Fabbri S.N.C. — Currently located in Concesio, Italy, Fabbri is the maker of one of the world's finest production over/under shotguns. In 1998, current retail prices started at $65,000, FOB Italy.

Fabrique Nationale — The large Belgian manufacturing facility where many Browning firearms have been made. See **Liège, Browning**.

Face — The upright portion of the breech of a side-by-side or over/under shotgun. It is against the face that the heads of the cartridges rest when the action is closed. A shotgun whose barrels have become loose through wear is often said to be "off the face."

False breech — The flat breech or action face of a double gun, through which the firing pins or strikers project. This term originally described the action of muzzleloading flint- and percussion-lock shotguns whose barrels had sealed breeches. A hook attached the barrels to the false breech, and a wedge through the fore-end held them in place. The false breech carried the locks, tumblers or hammers, trigger, and sears. See **action face, breech face, standing breech**.

False side plates — Decorative plates added to a boxlock action to mimic true sidelocks. False side plates serve primarily as an extended surface for engraving and serve no other purpose. A naive gun buyer might believe that a shotgun with false side plates is a sidelock gun. However, the absence of the pins or screws that hold the lock mechanism in a true sidelock should serve as a warning.

Federal Cartridge Company — Located in Anoka, Minnesota, Federal is one of the several major ammunition manufacturers in the United States.

Fences — The juncture between the flat areas of the action body and the rounded hemispheres or balls of the action that seal the breech end of the barrels.

Ferlach, Austria — A small village in south-central Austria where several gunmakers such as Winkler, Hofer, and Fanzoj work. They are mostly known for making combination guns such as drillings, but they will also make shotguns. At one time there were more than fifteen active gunmakers in Ferlach, but currently their number has dwindled to around half a dozen.

Field grade — A common identifier of the lowest grade of American-made shotgun. These guns usually have little or no engraving, but they often are of the same quality and have the same features as higher-grade models.

Field, The (Brit.) — The gun trials of 1858, '59, '66, and '75 were a series of public tests of muzzleloading and breechloading shotguns sponsored by the shooting newspaper *The Field*. These trials pitted the various shotguns against each other in terms of pattern percentage and shot penetration. All guns used the same relative ammunition. See **W. W. Greener,** *The Gun and Its Development.*

File-cut rib — The top surface of a rib that is hand-cut, matted, or serrated by means of a very fine file. Due to the labor-intensive nature of the work, only the very best, high-grade shotguns have file-cut ribs.

Finger groove — A wide, concave groove nearly the length of a shotgun's fore-end. It accommodates the shooter's fingertips, giving the shooter a better grip.

Finish — 1. The coating gunmakers apply to the wood and metal surfaces of a shotgun. Under normal circumstances the gunmaker will blue or blacken the metal surfaces and coat the wood with a lacquer, varnish, or oil to protect it from water. 2. A loose term indicating the appearance of both the metal and wood of a shotgun. See **bluing, linseed oil, oil finish**.

Fiocchi — An Italian-based ammunition company that sells its shotshells worldwide.

Firing pin — A cylindrical, semipointed steel pin that, when the tumbler or hammer hits it, strikes the primer, igniting the propellant and firing the chambered shotshell. Firing pins can be integral with the tumbler or hammer, or separate. See **striker**.

FITAS — Federation Internationale de Tir Aux Armes Sportives de Chasse, 10 Rue de Lisbonne, Paris, 75008, France. Of all the shotgunning sports, FITAS is the most challenging and most highly regulated of the various disciplines. Shot under strict rules, squads of up to six competitors shoot a prescribed set of stands in strict rotation. Competitors are required to hold their shotgun with the butt below the level of the armpit until the target is seen. In addition, changing of chokes is not allowed once the competitor is on the course. During competition, the squad first shoots all single targets, then they shoot combinations of the previously shot single targets as doubles. As in other sporting disciplines, all styles of clay targets are used. See **clay target**.

Fixed-breech — A single- or double-barrel shotgun. In a fixed-breech shotgun there are no moving parts other than the firing and locking mechanism, and the barrels lock into the standing breech during firing. Semiautomatic and pump-action shotguns are not fixed-breech firearms, because their locking mechanism moves within the action.

Flat-back action — An old style of sidelock action in which the wood of the buttstock does not extend to the fences but stops at a metal projection that is even with the rear of the bottom of the action, giving the gun a "flat back" appearance.

Fletch — A wooden buttstock blank of double thickness that the gunmaker reserves for building a true pair of best-quality shotguns. The assumption is that, when cut, the two halves will possess the same grain and weight.

Flintlock — The first really successful and economical firearms ignition system. A pair of adjustable jaws grasp a piece of flint at the top of the hammer. Below the hammer is the frizzen, a plate of steel against which the flint strikes, producing a shower of sparks that spew into a small pan containing very fine black powder located just below the frizzen. This priming powder burns through a small hole between the pan and the interior breech of the gun, igniting the main powder charge. The flintlock's relatively quick ignition of the powder charge made it possible to shoot flying birds. The flintlock was the pivotal system of ignition that led to the percussion cap, and ultimately to the breechloading shotgun of today.

Folding shotgun — A single-barrel shotgun that fully folds so that the barrel touches the belly or bottom of the buttstock. Upon unfolding, the breech goes into battery like any break-action shotgun. These guns are easy to transport in luggage or on a bicycle. Still manufactured in .410, a folding gun can be a handy camp gun for bird shooting. See **bicycle gun**.

Follower — The part of a magazine that is sandwiched between the magazine spring and the ammunition. In both a box magazine, such as that found on a bolt-action shotgun, or the more common tubular magazine found on pump and semiautomatic shotguns, the follower provides a smooth surface to rest against the unfired cartridges and, aided by the magazine spring, pushes the cartridges out of the magazine as the action cycles.

Following pair — Two clay targets that follow each other as rapidly as the trapper can recock the trap, place a clay target on the arm, and release the arm. See **sporting clays**.

Folsom, H. & D. — 312-14 Broadway, New York, New York. Importer and distributor of firearms from about 1890 to 1930, when they merged with Crescent-Davis, and then sold in 1954 to Universal Tackle and Sporting Goods Co. Far from complete, the following list includes brand and trade names of Crescent-made and Folsom-imported shotguns, all of which were inexpensive shotguns that constantly turn up in estates and at gun shows: American Gun Co., Bacon Arms, Baker Gun Co., T. Barker (for Sears), Carolina Arms Co., Central Arms Co., Cherokee Arms Co., Chesapeake Gun Co., Compeer, Cruso, Cumberland Arms Co., Elgin Arms Co., Elmira Arms Co., Empire Arms Co., Enders Oak Leaf, Enders Royal Service, Essex, Faultless, The Field, F. F. Forbes, C. W. Franklin, Harrison Arms Co., Hartford Arms Co., Harvard, Henry Gun Co., Hermitage Arms Co., Hermitage Gun Co., Howard Arms Co., Hummer, Interstate Arms Co., Jackson Arms Co., Kingsland Special, Kingsland 10 Star, Knickerbocker, Knox-All, Lakeside, J. H. Lau & Co., Leader Gun Co., Lee Special, Lee's Munner Special, Leige Arms Co., J. Manton & Co., Marshwood, Massachusetts Arms Co., Metropolitan, Minnesota Arms Co., Mississippi Valley Arms Co., Mohawk, Monitor, Wm. Moore and Co., Mt. Vernon Arms Co., National Arms Co., New Rival, New York Arms Co., Nitro Bird, Nitro Hunter, Norwich Arms Co., Not-Nac Manufacturing Co., Oxford Arms Co., C. Parker & Co., Peerless, Perfection, Piedmont,

Pioneer Arms Co., Quail, Queen City, Rev-O-Noc, W. Richards (not related to the British gunmaker Westley Richards), Richter, Rickard Arms Co., Royal Service, Rummel, Shue's Special, Sickel's Arms Co., Southern Arms Co., Special Service, Spencer Gun Co. Sportsmen, Springfield Arms Co., Square Deal, Stanley, State Arms, H. J. Sterling, St. Louis Arms Co., Sullivan Arms Co., Ten Star, Ten Star Heavy Duty, Tiger, Triumph, U.S. Arms Co., Victor, Victor Special, Virginia Arms Co., Volunteer, Vulcan Arms Co., Warren Arms Co., Wilkinson Arms Co., Wilmont Arms Co., Wilshire Arms Co., Wiltshire Arms Co., Winfield Arms Co., Winoca Arms Co., Wolverine, and Worthington Arms Co.

Foot position — The key to good shotgun marksmanship is good foot position. Foot position governs the ability of the body to swing on a target. American shotgunners typically adopt a rifleman's stance and foot position, in which the feet are at nearly a 90-degree angle to the flight path of the target; this position severely cramps the swing to the left for a right-handed shooter, and to the right for a left-handed shooter. Good shotgunning technique places the feet slightly to the right or parallel with the target's flight path (slightly to the left for a left-handed shooter). That position frees the swing. Foot position is a basic fundamental that shooting instructors teach as the foundation to good shotgunning technique.

Forcing cone — A tapered section of a shotgun barrel that serves as a transitional area from larger to smaller bore diameters. There are two forcing cones in most shotgun barrels. The primary forcing cone is immediately forward of the chamber. The second forcing cone is near the muzzle, where the cylinder bore meets the choke; this choke forcing cone helps the transition of the shot column into the tighter choke area. In shotgun barrels designed prior to the advent of plastic, gas-sealing wads, and for those that still embrace SAAMI standards that continue to reflect bores manufactured to shoot cartridges loaded with card and felt wads, the chamber forcing cones are quite abrupt and very short, measuring from ³/₈ to slightly less than ½ inch in length and having a 5- to 7-degree taper. Contemporary thinking and design recommends chamber forcing cones measuring between 1½ and 3 inches in length, providing a much longer and more gentle transition for the shot column and leading to better downrange performance. Research indicates that chamber forcing cones longer than three inches do not provide any additional benefit. See **bore**.

Forearm — The forward part of a one-piece stock.

Fore-end — The forward grip of a two-piece stock. Gunmakers normally make fore-ends of wood, but they may use graphite or plastic. The fore-end provides the grip for the forward hand and can be of several styles. The most common in double guns is the splinter fore-end, which is not really a grip but rather encases the ejector mechanism and fore-end iron that holds the shotgun together. The beavertail fore-end is larger and flatter on the bottom and extends up the sides of the barrels. Repeating shotguns, pumps, and semiautomatics tend to have semibeavertail fore-ends that provide a good grip for the pump-action

Fore-end: *Two styles of side-by-side fore-ends, the traditional splinter in the foreground and the American-style beavertail in the background.*

shotgun and that cover the gas-operating or recoil system of the semiautomatic. See **beavertail fore-end**.

Fore-end finial — A small, decorative addition to the very tip of the fore-end. In double shotguns having an Anson-style release, the finial contains the fore-end-release rod.

Fore-end iron — The metal portion of a double gun within the fore-end that contains the latch holding the fore-end assembly to the barrels and the moving parts of the ejectors.

Fore-end latch — The device that holds the fore-end to the barrels of a double gun. These latches take on several styles, the most common being the Anson, developed by William Anson and patented in 1873, which uses a pushrod that projects through the front tip of the fore-end. Others use spring-loaded catches that release by means of rotating a serrated latch or pushing a button; another is the Deeley and Edge type, which employs a lever on the bottom of the fore-end that pivots downward. Less expensive doubles often have fore-end latches that permit the fore-end to be snapped on and off.

Fore-end loop/fastener — A downward projection that gunmakers solder to the underside of a pair of barrels to engage the fore-end latch, keeping the barrels and forearm in firm contact.

Deeley and Edge improved fore-end.

Anson fore-end.

Grip fore-end.

Fore-end fasteners: Of the many fore-end fasteners introduced, the Deeley and Edge is the most in favor, owing to its handiness and neat appearance. The Anson patent bolt consists of an iron rod tube, kept in position by a spiral spring. The grip fore-end fastener is of a similar construction to the original Lefaucheux lever used in breechloading guns to secure the barrels.

Fork — A device used to measure barrel thickness. It consists of upright stems, one fixed and the other movable and attached to a micrometer dial, over which the barrel is slipped. When the barrel is moved the dial will register the wall thickness.

Forsyth, The Rev. Alexander — The recognized inventor of the percussion system of igniting powder in firearms. Forsyth received a patent for his percussion system on 11 April 1807. Others had developed similar systems, but Forsyth was the first to register his invention. His percussion cap, using fulminate of mercury, changed the manner of ignition of the main powder charge. Because the cap fits tightly over a nipple, there is less exposure to the elements. Ignition became far more reliable than it had been with flint ignition, in which the priming powder lies in a pan exposed to the weather. See **percussion cap**.

Four-gauge — A shotgun whose bore diameter permits the passage of four lead balls of equal size cast from one pound of lead. The bore diameter of a 4-gauge shotgun is 1.052 inches. See **gauge**.

.410-bore — The only shotgun currently produced whose bore is actually expressed as a caliber. Expressed as a gauge, the .410 would be a 67-gauge. Many think of the .410 as a gun for beginners because of its light recoil. However, because of the very small shot charge, ½ ounce in the 2½-inch shell to only $^{11}/_{16}$ ounce in the 3-inch hull, the .410 is really a gun for an expert shot. Some cite the gun's very light recoil, and, indeed, there are highly experienced shooting instructors who use .410s with beginners. But the beginning shooter is generally far better off with the 28-gauge, which offers a solid ¾-ounce load and, because of its larger frame, better handling characteristics. In the hands of a trained, experienced, and otherwise excellent shot, the .410 can produce good results; in the hands of a beginner, it can lead only to frustration.

Forward allowance (Brit.) — Another term for lead. See **lead**.

Foster, William Harnden — The American grouse hunter who wrote *New England Grouse Shooting,* but who is most famous for co-inventing the game of skeet. In order to practice the difficult shots he encountered in the grouse woods, and to keep in shape during the off season, Foster and his friend Charles E. Davies devised "shooting around the clock." It employed a single clay-pigeon thrower or trap at the 12 o'clock position with equally spaced shooting positions around a fifty-yard circle; he later reduced the circle to forty yards. When a neighbor complained, Davies and Foster cut the circle in half and added a second trap at 6 o'clock, later raising one of the traps to about ten or twelve feet off the ground. The result is today's skeet layout. See **skeet**.

Foster-style slug — A single lead projectile for big-game hunting with a shotgun, this slug is adequate to take white-tailed deer, European boar, black bear, and other light big game. The Foster-style slug has a series of riflinglike grooves in the sides of the slug that cause the slug to spin, and they perhaps impart some stability. These slugs are safe for use with any modern shotgun barrel but are most accurate in cylinder bores. The accurate range of the Foster-style slug is about fifty yards. See **rifled slug, slug**.

Four-barrel set — An over/under shotgun for American skeet shooting that has a single receiver and four separate sets of barrels in 12, 20, 28, and .410-bore. There are also game-gun multibarrel sets, but seldom do these encompass the four gauges; instead, they are normally two-gauge sets (12- and 20-gauge, 20- and 28-gauge) or barrels of different length and choke within the same gauge.

Fox, A. H. — Maker of one of America's classic side-by-side shotguns. In 1898, Ansley H. Fox bought several patents from the National Gun Company and founded the Fox Gun Company, which ultimately became A. H. Fox. Ansley Fox left the original company in 1900 and then opened the Philadelphia Gun Company in 1902. He left that company in 1904, and ultimately opened the A. H. Fox Gun Company in 1905. Fox bought out the Philadelphia Gun Company in 1906. By 1912 the A. H. Fox Gun Company was in receivership and the controlling interest was bought by brothers Edward and Clarence Godshalk. In November 1929, Savage Arms Company purchased Fox and continued to manufacture the line until the outbreak of World War II. Following the war, guns were assembled from parts, and the A. H. version of the Fox disappeared from the market. Savage manufactured the Fox Model B for many years, but it was in no way like the true A. H. Fox shotgun.

The Fox shotgun was of a simple design that yielded a highly reliable shotgun with a reputation for almost never breaking. The lockup is by means of a top lever that operates a rotating bolt, which engages an extension projecting from between the barrels. Because of its design, the bolt simply turned a bit more as the union wore. The action incorporated integral firing pins that also never failed. Forged as part of the tumbler or hammer, integral firing pins are not subjected to the same strains as independent firing pins or strikers and hence seldom break. This system also eliminates several parts, adding to its simplicity. The Fox shotgun was produced in many graded versions, some with lavish engraving. The Fox shotgun most likely to be encountered today is the

Sterlingworth, which, though plain, is mechanically the same as any other Fox, and is still to be found at semi-bargain prices. Currently, the Connecticut Shotgun Manufacturing Company in New Britain, Connecticut, manufactures a limited number of shotguns of the Fox design. For historical information on original Fox shotguns, contact Mr. John Callahan 53 Old Quarry Road, Westfield, MA 01085 U.S.A. There is a nominal charge (fifteen dollars as of 1999) per gun for historical research by Callahan. See **Connecticut Shotgun Manufacturing Company, Galazan.**

Frame — The action of a shotgun. The portion containing the firing and, in the case of repeating shotguns, the feeding mechanism. See **action.**

Franchi, Luigi — Manufacturer of sporting arms in Brescia, Italy, since 1860. With the discontinuation of the Browning Auto-5, Franchi is the last manufacturer to make a long-recoil-operated semiautomatic shotgun. They also make double shotguns as well as a gas-operated semiautomatic.

Francotte, Auguste & Cie. S.A. — Located in Liège, Belgium, since 1805, Francotte makes top-of-the-line side-by-side shotguns. V. L. & A. and Abercrombie and Fitch imported them from about 1900 through 1962. V. L. & A. is no longer in business and Abercrombie and Fitch no longer sells guns. See **Abercrombie and Fitch.**

Frizzen — In a flintlock gun, the upright projection of the pan cover against which the flint carried by the hammer strikes, causing a shower of sparks to drop into the primed pan, firing the gun.

Front-action sidelock — A sidelock gun in which the mainspring is in front of the hammer or tumbler. The front-action is the most common of sidelocks, and most contemporary sidelock shotguns are of this style. See **bar-in-wood, bar lock, sidelock.**

F

Fulminate of mercury — The priming compound common in percussion caps and early shotshells. Extremely corrosive, it accounted for most of the barrel pitting in shotguns up to the adoption of noncorrosive priming mixtures and beyond, because many corrosively primed shells remained in stock and in shooter's hands. See **pitting**.

Furniture (Brit.) – A term that refers to any adornments or additions to the stocks of a shotgun—that is, buttplates, pistol-grip caps, ovals, or any part that requires bluing such as the trigger guard, triggers, trigger plate, or fore-end iron.

Fuste (Ital.) — "Fore-end."

G

Galazan, Antony — Owner and manufacturer of the current production A. H. Fox shotgun by the Connecticut Shotgun Manufacturing Company. Galazan also manufactures a high-grade over/under under his name and issues an extensive catalog of shotgun parts and accessories.

Game book (Brit.) — A record book that individuals, clubs, or estates maintain for recording, by species, the game that hunters bag each shooting or hunting day. These books are wonderful historical records that contain references to famous hunters, game numbers, and other hunting ephemera.

Game calls — Instruments used to lure various game birds and animals to the gun by mimicking their calls. With the proper technique, waterfowl—ducks and geese—can be called successfully with mouth-blown calls made of wood or synthetic material, containing a reed or reeds. Turkey calls can be operated by mouth or activated by means of friction. One type of friction call is a box call with a sliding lid that rubs against one wall of the resonating chamber. Other turkey calls are circular with tops made of slate, glass, or synthetic material. These calls are operated by using a slim "striker" that is rubbed across the surface of the slate. Predators such as fox or coyote respond to calls that mimic the distress sounds of a dying rabbit. Male white-tailed deer respond, during the rut or breeding season, to the sound of antlers being clashed together to simulate two bucks fighting, or to a very soft, low-pitched grunt that resembles the sound of a buck trying to mate with a doe. In recent years, goose, turkey, and duck calls have become collectors' items—especially the early duck calls attributed to pioneering makers such as Victor Glodo, J. T. Beckhart, and Olt.

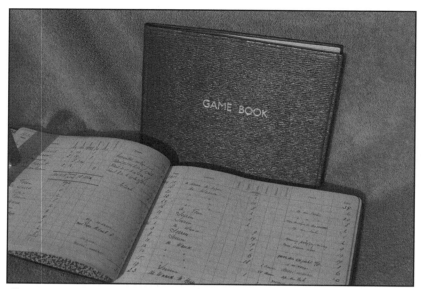

Game book: Game books are used to record the date and type of game bagged as well as general notes on the hunt. Often used in Europe, they are now in vogue in the United States.

Game calls: In addition to duck and goose calls, a crow call and box-style turkey call are shown. Crow hunting is a sport in itself, but the crow call is also used to rouse male turkeys (gobblers) and cause them to reveal their location so that hunters can move close to them and then call them to the gun with a box or other turkey call.

In the United States, calling contests are popular. Before a panel of knowledgeable judges, contestants use a series of calls that simulate the calling of a flock of ducks or geese or the call of a turkey during the spring mating season. The judges score the contestants on the quality of their calling.

Game carrier — A device used to carry bagged game birds. In the carrier—most commonly made of leather or a

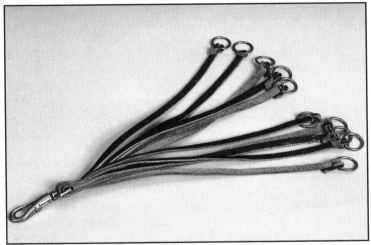

Game carrier: *A game carrier used to carry a number of birds by inserting their heads through the leather loops.*

combination of canvas and metal—the bird's head is snared in a loop that holds it securely for transportation in or from the field.

Game Conservancy, The — An organization that works for habitat acquisition and improvement, and the promotion of the shooting sports. Contact them at Burgate Manor, Fordingbridge, Hants SP6 1EF, U.K.

Game counter (Brit.) — A device to count the game birds and animals hunters shoot.

Game gun (Brit.) — Any shotgun for shooting game birds, as distinct from a shotgun specifically for skeet, trap, or sporting clays.

Garden gun (Brit.) — A very small-bore shotgun, traditionally a 9.1mm, useful only for shooting pests around the home or garden.

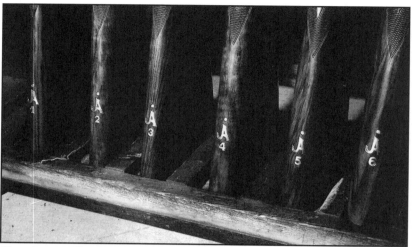

Garniture: *Six AyA shotguns of identical bore, choke, and dimensions are being readied for delivery.*

Garniture (Brit.) — A matched trio of shotguns specifically for shooting driven game. Although rare today, during the golden age of driven game shooting, many of the top shots owned and used garnitures.

Garwood, G. T. — Best known as Gough Thomas, the late Gough Thomas Garwood was the gun editor for the British publication *Shooting Times*. Trained as a civil engineer, Garwood wrote insightful columns that shed light on many facets of British shotgunning. He also prepared several books containing reprints of his *Shooting Times* columns.

Gas-operated — A style of semiautomatic repeating shotgun that uses some of the propellant gases to cycle the action. Upon firing, some of the high-pressure gases generated by the burning of the powder bleed off through one or two ports that pierce the bottom of the barrel, approximately five to seven inches forward of the chamber mouth. These gases flow into the piston area. When the pressure rises to a sufficient level, the piston drives rearward.

The action of the piston imparts motion to some manner of linkage—action bar, or sleeve—that in turn drives the breechbolt to the rear. During the rearward movement of the breechbolt, the extractor strips the fired hull from the chamber, and, near the end of the breechbolt's travel, the ejector expels the hull. If there is no fresh cartridge in the magazine, the breechbolt locks to the rear, the action remaining open. If there is an unfired shell available, the magazine releases it as the breechbolt reaches the end of its travel. As the fresh shell leaves the magazine, the breechbolt lock trips and it moves forward, tripping the carrier dog; that causes the carrier to rise, bringing the fresh round up to the level of the

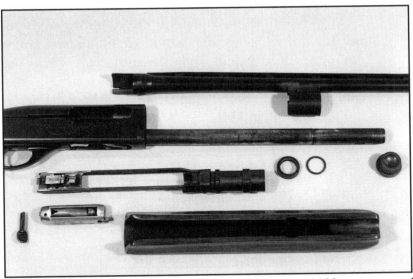

Gas-operated: The working parts of a Remington 1100 gas-operated semiautomatic shotgun. Top to bottom: The barrel with the gas cylinder through which the gas enters the piston; the receiver and attached magazine tube around which the piston and inertia sleeve move. (Left to right) The action bar and attached inertia sleeve; the piston rings and neoprene piston seal and magazine cap; operating handle, breechbolt, and fore-end.

empty chamber. The breechbolt drives it home, and the extractor snaps over the rim. See **action bar, autoloader, breechbolt, ejector, extractor**.

Gas port — One or two small-diameter holes in the bottom of the barrel of a gas-operated semiautomatic shotgun through which propellant gases flow in order to operate the action.

Gas vent valve — A small port in the sides of the action balls through which hot propellant gases that result from the piercing of a primer or failed case can escape. See **vented breech**.

Gatillo (Sp.) — "Trigger."

Gauge — The common method of expressing the bore diameter of a shotgun. Historically, the term refers to the number of equal-size balls cast from one pound of lead that would pass through a barrel of a specific diameter. Therefore, the 10-gauge's bore would allow ten lead balls of equal size to pass through; the 12-gauge, twelve balls; and so forth. The 16-gauge is perhaps the easiest to envision, because it is the gauge that would accommodate sixteen one-ounce lead balls. Today, manufacturers still use gauges but use decimal measurements to identify choke constrictions. The following are nominal bore diameters as specified by SAAMI. See **SAAMI**.

4-gauge	1.052 inches
6-gauge	0.919 inch
8-gauge	0.835 inch
10-gauge	0.775 inch
12-gauge	0.729 inch
16-gauge	0.665 inch
20-gauge	0.615 inch
28-gauge	0.550 inch
.410-bore	0.410 inch

Ghost-ring sight — A rear, aperture-style sight in use by police and military SWAT teams. Turkey hunters also use the ghost-ring sight. This style of sight provides quick but more critical shot placement than is possible with standard rib and bead sights.

Glass ball traps — One of the earliest forms of trapshooting. A transitional target between live pigeons and the clay target of today, the targets were glass balls sometimes filled with feathers or soot and thrown by specially made traps.

Glasses, shooting — Eyeglasses that ride high on the face and have specially hardened lenses to protect the shooter from ricochets, slapping brush, or bits of clay targets. Lenses are available in a rainbow of colors that make it easier to see clay targets against

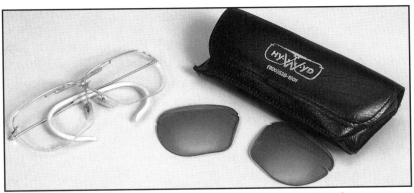

Glasses: In all shooting it is strongly recommended that shooters wear shooting glasses as protection against ricochets, broken clay-target fragments, and the like. Here is an example of a pair of shooting glasses that features interchangeable lenses.

specific backgrounds or that mute the background to make game animals or birds more recognizable. Shooting glasses should be a part of every shotgunner's kit. Wear them whenever you engage in shooting of any kind. See **eye protection**.

Goose gun — Any large-gauge, tightly choked shotgun appropriate for shooting large geese. Often, but not always, these guns have long barrels.

Goose load — A shotshell that makes use of large-size shot— No. 2 lead, BB lead; No. 2 or BB bismuth; No. 1 or BB tungsten/polymer; No. 1 steel, BB, BBB, T, or F steel. Goose loads are intended for hunting Canada geese.

Grade — A term that describes the quality of wood used for the buttstock and forearm of a shotgun, and the amount and style of its engraving. "Field grade" guns often make use of rather plain wood, normally American black walnut or a hardwood with little or no fancy grain, and usually have little engraving save the manufacturer's name or trademark. Some field-grade shotguns do have impressed or rolled engraving, but don't confuse that with high-quality hand engraving. Manufacturers give higher-grade shotguns various names, and the firearms possess mainly walnut stocks of increasing beauty of grain and more elaborate engraving in ever-larger coverage as the grade increases. It should be borne in mind, however, that high-grade shotguns are often little more than a prettier version of the same field-grade gun.

Grain — The distinguishing feature of any wooden stock. To have the very best characteristics for a shotgun buttstock, the grain should run lengthwise from the head of the stock through the hand or grip area. On inexpensive buttstocks, the grain continues without any particular features, save the dark and light lines of the wood. Higher-grade stocks possess varying degrees of fancy grain, such as feathering. Many stock-makers prefer French or Circassian walnut for its hard composition, although most stocks are of American black walnut. Black

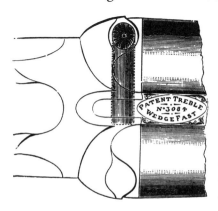

walnut can possess exquisitely figured grain but is not as hard as French or Circassian walnut. See **buttstock, Circassian.**

Greener crossbolt — One of many locking mechanisms that can hold the barrels to the action of a double shotgun. The Greener crossbolt consists of a tapered, hardened pin that is fitted crosswise through the top of the action; generally, the top

Greener crossbolt: *This W. J. Jeffery game gun uses a Greener-style crossbolt as a third fastener. It also has a Purdey-style double underbolt, making it an extremely solid shotgun.*

lever moves it to the left. There is a mating opening in projection at the top and between the barrels that fits into a similarly shaped opening in the top of the action. When closed, the extension fits into its recess and the pin slides through the opening in the extension, providing a tight lockup. See **top lever.**

Greener's rule of ninety-six — Greener stated that a shotgun should be ninety-six times heavier than the weight of the shot charge it fires in order to ensure the shooter's comfort and the longevity of the gun. Using this rule, a shotgun firing 1 ounce of shot should weigh at least 6 pounds; 6¾ pounds for a shotgun firing 1¹/₈ ounces of shot; 7½ pounds for 1¼ ounces, and so on. Of the many various pronouncements made by early gunmakers, this one remains true.

Greener side safety — An invention by W. W. Greener that moved the safety catch from atop the top strap behind the top lever to the side of the action within the side panel. Slid front to back, this safety was solely on guns of Greener's manufacture,

Greener Side Safety: *The Greener side safety is popular on Continental guns, especially drillings, which use the Greener safety for "fire" and "safe" and the top tang safety to control the rifle barrel.*

and it is awkward compared with the rather simple and straightforward operation of the conventional-style safety catch mounted on the top strap. See **safety, top strap**.

Greener, William Wellington — (1834–1921) One of the leading Birmingham gunmakers, who patented several devices, including the Greener crossbolt locking mechanism and the Greener side safety. The Greener factory, established in the 1800s, is still in operation, although no U.S. importer currently handles Greener shotguns. William Greener is perhaps most famous as the author of *The Gun and Its Development*, first published in 1881, which stretched to more than nine editions, the latter considered the best. *The Gun and Its Development* traces the history and development of firearms and gives insights into firearm construction and proofing, along with much ephemera of interest to shotgunners. It is currently available on the used-book market.

Gresham, Grits (Claude) — For many years the shooting editor of *Sports Afield,* Grits Gresham and his son Tom have brought shooting to the public through their weekly television and radio programs, which deal strictly with shooting and the shooting sports. The elder Gresham has published several books on American hunting, and the father and son have collaborated on a number of additional outdoor books. Gresham was trained as a wildlife manager and began writing when he worked for the Louisiana Fish and Game Department, using his extensive background and in-the-field experiences for material. In addition to his writing, television, and radio work, he appeared in a series of humorous Miller Lite beer commercials that aired during the 1970s.

Griffin & Howe — Founded in New York City in 1923 by Seymour Griffin and James Howe, this firm made its name by building custom rifles. Griffin & Howe continues to offer top-notch gunsmithing services and carries a large inventory of fine shotguns. Currently Griffin & Howe has two locations, one in New York City and the other, where they do their gunsmith-

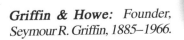

Griffin & Howe: *Founder, Seymour R. Griffin, 1885–1966.*

ing work, in Bernardsville, New Jersey, about a thirty-minute drive from Manhattan.

Griffschale (Ger.) — "Grip."

Grilletto (Ital.) — "Trigger."

Grip — The area of the buttstock immediately behind the action, where the shooter's trigger hand grasps the stock. The grip—or hand, as the British prefer to call it—can take on a variety of shapes that begin with the straight grip and slowly add arc or curve through the half-pistol grip and the Prince of Wales grip to the full pistol grip favored by Americans and those who shoot skeet, trap, and sporting clays. Grips commonly have an oval cross section; some straight grips, however, have a four-pointed diamond cross section and are called diamond grips. See **diamond hand, half-pistol grip, hand, pistol grip, Prince of Wales grip, straight stock**.

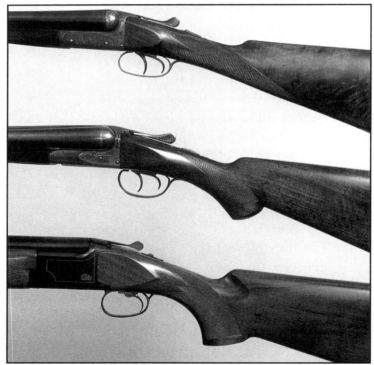

Grip: *The three styles of grip or hand.* **(Top to bottom)** *English or straight grip; semi-pistol grip; full pistol grip.*

Grip safety — A safety in a pistol-grip stock that the shooter squeezes to unblock the triggers and enable the shotgun to fire. This style of safety was never popular; in the 1890s, various makers used it on a very few shotguns.

Grulla Armas — Located in Eibar, Spain, Grulla is one of the top manufacturers of quality side-by-sides. There is a limited annual production.

Guancia (Ital.) — "Grip."

Gun fit — The most important aspect of any shotgun. Since the shooter of a shotgun does not aim the gun but rather points and swings on game and clay targets, the fit of the buttstock is vitally important. The fact that a shotgun must shoot where one looks directly translates to gun fit. If a shotgun does not fit, the shot charge can be off the target by several feet at extended ranges. The buttstock must fit so that the shot charge goes where the shooter is looking without any shifting or adjusting on the part of the shooter. See **cast off, cast on, comb, drop**.

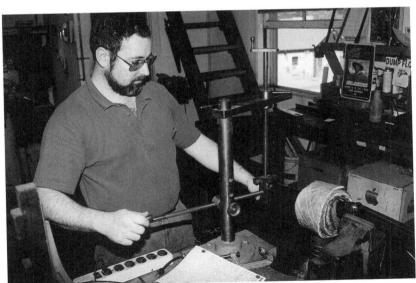

Gun fit: *A gunsmith at Griffin & Howe bends a shotgun stock to a customer's dimensions using a bending jig and hot oil, which softens the wood.*

Gun fit: *Ken Davies, Holland & Holland's senior shooting instructor, checks a student's buttstock against the try gun prior to suggesting changes to the stock.*

Gun safe — A burglar-proof and fireproof cabinet or safe for the storage of firearms.

Hagelvapnet (Sw.) — "Shotgun," in all its variations.

Hahn (Ger.) — "Hammer."

Halbautomatisch (Ger.) — "Semiautomatic."

Half-pistol grip — A style of hand or grip that is neither a full pistol grip nor a straight grip. A graceful design, it provides some of the hands-in-line feel of the straight grip along with some of the firmer grip that the full pistol grip offers. See **grip, hand.**

Hammer/tumbler — The part of the firing mechanism that actually strikes the firing pin. Hammer is the favored American word, while "tumbler" is preferred in Great Britain. Both terms describe the spring-driven part of the action that, upon release by the sear, pivots around its axis and strikes the firing pin. The pin then goes forward with sufficient force to crush the primer against the anvil, starting ignition of the chambered shotshell. On some shotguns, the Model 21 Winchester, Fox, and Remington 3200, for example, the firing pins are integral with the hammers, providing faster lock time and ignition and eliminating the breakage of separate firing pins. See **firing pin, integral firing pins, sear, striker.**

Hammerless — A term that describes any firearm that does not have an external, manually cocked hammer.

Hammer gun — A shotgun with external hammers that are manually cocked prior to firing. During the transitional period from exposed or external hammers to hammerless shotguns, some external hammer guns incorporated self-cocking external hammers, but such shotguns are rare.

Hand (Brit.) — The place where the shooter's trigger hand grips the buttstock. See **grip, stock.**

Hand guard — A leather-covered steel device that slips over the barrels of a side-by-side shotgun to insulate the shooter's leading hand from the heat generated by firing the gun. In shooting driven birds, skeet, trap, or sporting clays,

Hand guard: *(Above) A leather hand guard used on a side-by-side shotgun to insulate the shooter's hand from the hot barrels during extended shooting.* *(Below) A leather hand guard mounted on a set of barrels.*

in which shooters fire many shells in a short period of time, the barrels become quite hot. In the case of side-by-sides with splinter or wedge fore-ends, a hand guard is necessary. Never pick up a shotgun by the hand guard, as these commonly attach by friction only. Although they can mount with a catch that holds the hand guard firmly in place, it is usually easy for a guard to slip, causing a dropped gun and, potentially, an accidental discharge.

Handloading — Reloading of one's own ammunition. Clay-target shooters often do their own reloading as a means of saving money on ammunition. See **loader, reloading**.

Hare (Brit.) — Hares are a species similar to rabbits.

Harrington & Richardson — Manufacturer of utility firearms for over a century. Best known for inexpensive revolvers and single-barrel shotguns.

Hearing protection — The discharge of a shotgun creates sound levels in the range of 120 to 140 decibels, sufficient to cause permanent damage to various parts of the inner ear, resulting in hearing loss. Most clay ranges require shooters to wear hearing protection, and many hunters and driven game shooters wear hearing protection to avoid hearing damage. In the form of ear muffs that externally cover the ear or plugs that block the ear canal, either or both provide hearing protection. Ear plugs of disposable, soft foam expand to fill the ear canal; some shooters prefer to acquire custom-molded plugs. In addition, there are now ear plugs and muffs with internal electronics that make normal hearing possible but shut down when the sound intensity reaches a certain level. Most audiologists advise wearing both plugs and muffs.

Heel — The rearmost part of the top of the shotgun stock, where the comb and butt meet. It is here that the gunmaker takes one of the important dimensions in fitting a stock. See **drop at heel**.

Heel and toe plates — Steel plates inletted into the toe and heel of the butt whose function is to prevent splitting or other damage to these two delicate areas of the buttstock.

Herter's, Inc. — Located in Waseca, Minnesota, Herter's was a mail-order company that offered a complete line of adjustable chokes, ventilated ribs, finished and unfinished stocks, cleaning supplies, boots, clothing, and other shotgunning, shooting, and hunting-related paraphernalia. Initially noted for their low prices and high quality, they went out of business in the early 1970s, a demise that was largely the result of mismanagement. George Leonard Herter, who successfully managed Herter's, Inc., through about 1970, was one of the all-time great catalog writers. His descriptions of merchandise made Herter's seem the only supplier of quality products. A balding man of slight build who wore rather thick glasses, Herter never wanted to appear in photographs, lest his customers see him as something other than a second Paul Bunyan. In addition to making somewhat exaggerated claims, Herter also invented the "North Star Guide Association," a fictitious organization of equally fictitious Alaskan and Canadian guides who endorsed Herter's products.

Hide (Brit.) — A structure in which hunters conceal themselves when shooting wildfowl, crow, or pigeon. See **blind**.

Hinge pin — The round pin, also called a cross pin, that runs through the bar of the action and around which the barrels rotate. See **cross pin, trunnions**.

Holland & Holland — Founded in 1835 by the late Harris Holland, Holland & Holland is one of the great shotgun makers. Currently at 31-33 Bruton Street, Mayfair, London, as of 1998 they also had stores in New York and Paris; the factory is on Harrow Road in West London. In addition, H&H owns and operates a shooting grounds at Northwood, outside of London, and their instructors tour internationally offering shooting instruction. Although one of the old surviving gunmakers, Holland & Holland is now a subsidiary of the Chanel Group. They have, however, continued to expand their line of shotguns to include over/unders for sporting clays and game.

Holland & Holland: *The Holland & Holland gun room in their New York facility.*

Hollow rib – A rib found on side-by-side shotguns that lies between the barrels and is actually hollow. Hollow ribs can be either concave or flat. See **concave rib, rib**.

Hook — The circular cut in the barrel lumps that enables the barrels to mate with the hinge pin so that they can rotate open and closed.

Horns – Two thin columns of wood that form the two sides of the head of the buttstock of a sidelock shotgun. The top and bottom tangs and locks fit into the horns, so named because of their resemblance to gracefully curved animal horns.

Howdah gun — A two-barreled pistol of large bore (usually .577), a howdah gun looks like a very short-barreled shotgun. Intended to be used from a howda, or elephant seat, these guns were the final defense against an attacking tiger. Purdey, Holland & Holland, and other firms often made these guns to order; many were highly ornate.

Hunt, Ken — One of the world's great engravers, Ken Hunt works most often on double guns.

Hunt, Ken: *Ken at work on a sidelock.*

I

Importer's mark — In the United States, imported firearms must bear this mark, a stamp indicating the name of the individual or the company that imported the arm.

Inertia block — A device in some single-trigger double shotguns that both prevents doubling—firing of both barrels simultaneously—and also sets the trigger to fire the second barrel. When the shotgun recoils rearward the inertia block continues to the rear a short distance after the gun has itself stopped recoiling, momentarily disengaging the trigger from the sear or sear lifter. As it returns to engagement with the sear mechanism, it moves into position to engage the sear of the unfired barrel.

Inertia-operated — A style of semiautomatic shotgun that relies solely on the inertia principle to operate the mechanism. One could argue that all semiautomatic shotguns utilize inertia, and that is true. Gas-operated semiautos set the action into operation through the force of propellant gases acting on a piston, which transfers this force through a linkage to the breechbolt. The obsolescent Winchester Models 50 and 59 and Browning Double Automatic worked on the inertia principle, by using a short-recoiling slip chamber that traveled rearward but a fraction of an inch, imparting movement to the breechbolt. A heavy mass in the buttstock pulled the bolt rearward, cycling the action. The modern Benelli operates by means of inertia by first compressing a carefully calibrated spring through the use of an inertia mass that remains stationary through recoil; once the spring hits maximum compression, it forces the inertia mass to the rear, cycling the action.

Inlay — An object, most often of precious metal, that the gunmaker insets into the metal or stock of a shotgun. Inlays can be of animals, birds, or any other subjects that

Inlay: *A Purdey single-barrel trap gun, serial number 27175, with Ken Hunt's engraving and gold inlay of a thistle.*

suit the taste of the owner. High-quality shotguns often display exquisite inlay work, although the rather crude inlays from the Orient are far more common.

Inletting — The detailed and often delicate process of fitting a shotgun action into its stock. The very best inletting exhibits the same fine finish as does the exterior of the stock.

In-the-white — The time during the manufacture of a shotgun when all of the parts have been assembled, but the gunmaker has not yet engraved and blued the metal or shaped and finished the buttstock and fore-end for delivery. In this state it is a fully functional shotgun, merely unfinished. It is during this in-the-white stage that the stock and metal work receive final adjustments to ensure that the dimensions and choking are precisely to the customer's order. Often, guns will be left in-the-white to be finished to specification when a customer desires quick delivery.

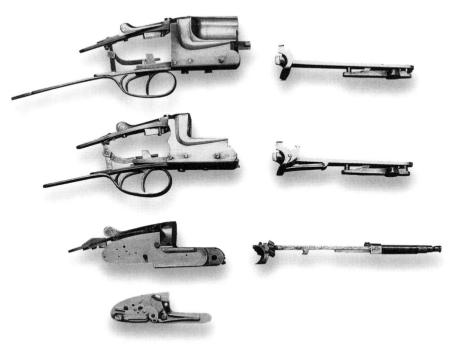

In-the-white

Insurance — Gun owners should carry insurance against theft and fire so that they can replace their firearms in the event of loss. Many national firearms organizations offer such insurance, and often homeowners and apartment dwellers can insure their firearms through their homeowner's or renter's policy. It is also advisable to carry some form of liability insurance to protect against financial liability in a shooting accident.

Integral firing pins — Firing pins that are made as a part of the hammer or tumbler. This style of firing pin, used, for example, in all A. H. Fox shotguns and in the Remington 3200 over/under, eliminates the need for separate strikers or firing pins, and is an almost indestructible design.

Interceptor/intercepting sear — Also called a second sear, this is a specific part of a sidelock or boxlock that ensures that should the primary sear be jarred out of engagement with the sear bent, the interceptor sear will grasp the tumbler or hammer and stop it from accidentally discharging the gun. During deliberate firing of the gun, the trigger simultaneously lifts both the primary and second or interceptor sears. Most recently Browning and U.S. Repeating Arms Company/ Winchester have applied this technology to the trigger of their Gold and Super X 2 semiautomatic shotguns, rendering them safer than repeating shotguns that simply use a crossbolt safety to block the rearward movement of the trigger. See **bent, sidelock.**

International Shooting Union — Because of its abbreviation, ISU, some people confuse this organization with the International Skating Union. The International Shooting Union is the regulating body for all international shooting competition. As such, it advises local Olympic committees on the correct setup for Olympic competition ranges and also sets up ranges for other international shooting meets. The ISU establishes and enforces the rules governing international shooting events.

International-style skeet — See **Olympic skeet**.

ISU — See **International Shooting Union**.

Ithaca, Ithacagun, Ithaca Acquisition Corporation — Another of the old American shotgun manufacturers who have fallen on hard times and been resuscitated. Ithaca originally made quality side-by-side shotguns, including the rare and exquisite Sousa Grade trap gun, named for America's March King, John Philip Sousa. Sousa, in addition to being America's best-known band composer, who led his professional concert band for forty years, was an enthusiastic trapshooter and hunter. As time passed, Ithaca began producing a bottom-ejecting pump-action repeater called the Model 37. For years this shotgun was the backbone of Ithaca's production. In 1975, with steel shot beginning to loom large, Ithaca produced the Mag 10, a semiautomatic shotgun designed to shoot the 3½-inch, 10-gauge magnum cartridge. Although initially flawed, the Mag 10 ultimately became a very successful shotgun, and when Ithaca went into receivership in the 1980s, Remington bought the patent rights. Now that the company has been reborn as Ithaca Acquisition Corporation, the Model 37 is again in production. See **Sousa**.

J

Jaeger (Ger.) — "Hunter."

Jones underlever — Patented by Birmingham, England, gunmaker Henry Jones, the Jones underlever is an extremely strong bolting mechanism. Many hammer guns used it prior to the development of the more common snap action. This style of locking uses a T-shaped rotating bolt that engages two opposing slots cut into the lumps. The bolt pulls the barrels down into firm engagement with the action bar. Even after the snap action came into use, manufacturers employed the Jones underlever on double rifles and big-bore shotguns because of its great strength. See **snap action.**

Jug choke — A type of choke cut into the area immediately behind the muzzle after the original choke has been removed. The jug choke is useful for shotguns whose muzzles have bulged, burst, or otherwise been damaged and the barrels cut off. By cutting a shallow depression in the barrel about an inch or two behind the muzzle, some choke can be restored. Today, with the advent of screw-in choke tubes, very few of these stopgap repairs are attempted; it is eminently more practical simply to install screw-in chokes.

Keeper's gun — Generally a lesser-priced boxlock kept and used by a gamekeeper to control vermin.

Kent-Gamebore Cartridge — With home offices near Toronto, Ontario, Canada, this is the company that developed the first successful tungsten-polymer nontoxic shot. A conglomerate of American and British manufacturing plants headquartered in Canada, Kent-Gamebore is one of the largest suppliers of shotgun cartridges in Europe.

Kimble, Fred — (ca. 1850-1930) The Illinois duck hunter attributed with the discovery of chokeboring. In truth, while it is possible that Fred Kimble may have furthered the use of chokeboring in the United States, this attribution is mostly folklore. W. W. Greener, in his extensive book *The Gun and Its Development*—first published in 1881, about the time that Kimble is said to have discovered chokeboring—gives credit to an American gunsmith named Sylvester Roper, who used screw-on rings of various constrictions at the muzzle. Roper received his patent on 10 April 1866. Furthermore, Greener cites J. W. Long, who, in his book *American Waterfowling,* credits Jeremiah Smith of Southfield, Rhode Island, "who discovered its [chokeboring's] merits in 1827."

There is no dispute that Kimble was a market hunter, an excellent shot, an innovator, and someone who wrote about his life's work, but while he certainly did some work to further the practice of chokeboring, the evidence points elsewhere as to its invention. Kimble's date of birth is unknown, but he was recorded as still alive as late as the latter part of the 1920s. Considering that he could have lived into his eighties, that he was market hunting and working on chokebored shotguns in the 1870s, and that Nash Buckingham wrote of a "delightful

Kimble, Fred: *Fred Kimble is frequently credited with discovering chokeboring of shotgun barrels. Although he used chokebored shotguns as a market hunter, evidence suggests that Sylvester Roper and others had developed choke devices before any of Kimble's claims. His discovery was neither patented nor documented, but folklore continues to perpetuate the legend that he discovered choke.*

and voluminous correspondence . . . when at an advanced age, he was living in retirement in California," it is possible that Kimble was born between 1850 and 1860.

Kiplauf (Ger.) — "Tipping barrel." See **break-top action**.

Knuckle — The rounded portion of the front of the action bar through which the cocking levers protrude and against which the fore-end iron rests and rotates.

Kolben (Ger.) — "Butt."

Krieghoff, H., Gun Co. — Established in 1886 in Suhl, Germany, Krieghoff currently manufactures its fine shotguns in Ulm, Germany. Noted as top-of-the-line skeet and trap guns, their high-quality sporting over/unders, double rifles, and drilling often escape the attention of prospective buyers.

L

Laminated steel barrel — Another term for a twist or Damascus barrel. See **Damascus barrel, twist barrel**.

Laminated stock — A buttstock constructed of alternating layers of different woods or synthetics. Gluing the layers together and curing the stock under heat and pressure yields a buttstock of great strength and dimensional stability but of little beauty.

Lancaster, Charles — (d. 1847) A British gunmaker whose company eventually amalgamated with Stephen Grant and Joseph Lang, later Atkin, Grant, and Lang, and ultimately Atkin, Grant, Lang, and Churchill, which ceased business in 1980. Charles William Lancaster, the founder's son, was the author of *The Art of Shooting*, one of several texts by the well-known gunmakers of the time on how to shoot and other shotgunning lore. Lancaster's text went through at least twelve editions, of which the twelfth appeared in 1954. In the preface to the ninth edition, Grant and Lang state that Lancaster published *The Art of Shooting* in 1889, although Geoffrey Boothroyd states in his book *Boothroyd's Revised Directory of British Gunmakers* that Charles Lancaster died in 1878; it is possible that publication took place after Lancaster's death.

Lap — To finely grind or finish. Gunmakers lap the interior of barrels to their finished dimensions and polish. For the finest barrels, the gunmaker laps using a lead lap and a very fine abrasive lapping compound, inserting the lap into the barrel and drawing it back and forth so as to polish the barrels lengthwise. When the lap becomes loose, the gunmaker withdraws and replaces it with a larger-diameter one, recoating it with the abrasive compound, and again draws it through the barrels to create the proper finish. The use of a rotary lap charged with lapping compound is common for less expensive barrels. The powered, rotary lap produces a high polish quickly and easily, but the slower hand method yields a superior finish.

Lauf (Ger.) – "Barrel."

Lead — The term that describes how a shooter maneuvers a shotgun so as to hit a flying target. It is the very essence of wingshooting. Another term for lead is forward allowance, which better describes the technique.

Lead shot — The original and most ballistically sound projectile for use in shotguns. During its fabrication, molten lead is poured through a sieve at the top of a seven-story, 150-foot-high tower. The sieve contains holes of precise size to form pellets of specific dimensions. The lead is alloyed with 0.5 to 7 percent antimony, which acts as a surfactant, causing sufficient surface tension to form the pellets into perfect spheres. During the drop, the lead-antimony pellets partially harden, and the hardening completes as the pellets plunge into a pool of water at the bottom of the tower. Following dropping, the pellets roll over a series of plates between which is a gap. Round pellets gather sufficient speed to be able to jump the gaps; deformed and out-of-round pellets cannot roll as quickly and drop through the gaps, ready for remelting. See **soft shot.**

During the 1970s until about 1985, lead shot came increasingly under fire as the cause of lead poisoning in dabbling ducks, those that feed from shallow ponds, lakes, and sloughs where spent lead shot is present. Currently, in the United States it is unlawful to hunt waterfowl with lead shot. Equally in Europe, lead shot has come under scrutiny and has been banned in some countries for waterfowl hunting. See **bismuth shot, dropped shot, nontoxic shot, soft shot, tungsten/polymer shot.**

Lebeau-Courally — High-quality double shotgun and rifle maker, founded in 1865, based in Liège, Belgium. Their products are considered among the best of continental Europe. Rue Saint-Gilles 386, Liège, Belgium, B-4000.

Leg-of-mutton — A style of case that looks like the leg of an animal. Made of hard, thick leather, the case has two or three compartments inside; one is for the action and the other for the barrel or barrels. A sturdy end-flap closes the case. A very popular style during the first half of the twentieth century, the leg-of-mutton case (also called a "Hurlingham case"), while still made, has slipped greatly in popularity in favor of much stronger and more practical aluminum and composite cases.

Length of pull — 1. The distance between the front trigger of a double-trigger gun (or the trigger of a single-trigger gun) and the center of the buttstock. 2. One of the critical measurements for fitting a stock, which takes into account the length of the shooter's arms and general physical build. British gun fitters also reflect the angle of pitch as a measurement of the length of pull taken at toe, center, and heel of the buttstock. See **buttstock, heel, toe, pitch.**

Liège, Belgium — The center of arms manufacturing in Belgium. In addition to some smaller gunmakers, the giant Fabrique Nationale works is in Herstal, a suburb of Liège. Fabrique Nationale produces an extensive line of firearms, and it has also manufactured firearms for Browning.

Lifter action — See **push-button opener.**

Lifting plate — Another term for trigger blade, which is the part of the trigger that lifts the sear from engagement with the hammer.

Linseed oil — One of the oldest finishes for gunstocks; gunstock makers often use linseed oil as a finish for fine shotguns. It is normal to mix linseed oil, a derivative of flaxseed, with a drying agent and often a coloring agent such as alkanet root, which provides a red color, then apply it in thin coats with considerable drying time between applications. Building up a linseed oil finish takes several weeks. The finish is not impervious to wet weather, but it is easy to repair; rubbing on a thin coat of oil will quickly cover minor scratches. Many gunstock makers currently seal their stocks with a hard, synthetic sealer, then apply a linseed-oil finish over the sealer, thus providing both the warm glow of an oil finish and a weatherproof underlayment. See **finish**.

Ljutic, Al — The Yakima, Washington, shooter who designed and manufactured a shotgun for trapshooters that uses an opener located in the front of the trigger guard.

Loader — 1. In driven game-bird shooting, an assistant who stands just behind and to the side of the shooter to load one gun of a pair while the shooter fires the other at approaching game. When the shooter is using a single gun—it is always a double—the loader recharges the chambers so the shooter can keep his eyes on the flight of the birds. 2. A term designating the press or machine used by handloaders to reload ammunition. See **handloading, reloading**.

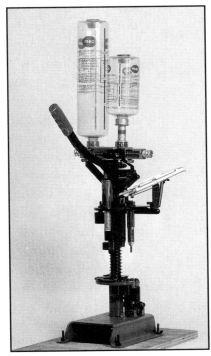

Loader: This shotshell loader by MEC enables the shotgunner to assemble excellent handloads for field and target shooting.

Lock — The complete mechanism that carries the tumbler or hammer, tumbler or hammer spring, and sear(s). This term is unique to double guns; repeaters use the term "trigger group" to delineate their locks. The term "lock" is most common as part of a compound word: flintlock, boxlock, or sidelock. See **boxlock, droplock, flintlock, sidelock, trigger group**.

Lock time — The amount of time, in milliseconds, between the pull of the trigger and the firing of the shell. Shotguns with strikers or firing pins integral with the hammer (such as the Winchester Model 21, Fox, or Remington 3200) have faster lock times, as there is no firing-pin or striker travel to account for. In calculating lead for moving targets, the shooter must account for both lock time as well as the muzzle-to-target time; that is why follow-through is important for consistent results. See **lead**.

Locking block — 1. The portion of the breechbolt of a repeating shotgun (that is, a pump or semiautomatic) that engages the locking recess in the frame or barrel extension, locking the bolt to the rear of the chamber. It is this locking block in consort with the breechbolt and its engagement with the locking recess in the frame or barrel extension that takes the force of ignition upon firing. 2. A term that some use to describe, although somewhat incorrectly, the sliding Purdey-style underbolt. See **barrel extension, battery, breechbolt, locking recess, underbolt**.

Locking bolt — Another term for a Purdey-style underbolt.

Locking lugs — 1. The notches cut into the barrel lumps that engage a sliding underbolt, holding the gun tightly closed when in battery. 2. The projections that some semiautomatic shotguns employ on rotary locking bolts. See **lump, underbolt**.

Locking recess — 1. The area into which the locking block engages when a firearm is in battery. 2. In the Winchester Model 12 pump-action shotgun, the locking recess is a cut made in the top of the receiver that engages the rear of the breechbolt when the gun is in battery.

London best — The term most often applied to a bespoke or custom shotgun of the highest quality, made in London, England.

London Proof House — Established in 1637 to ensure the safety of firearms, the London Proof House tests all firearms with cartridges that have been loaded to produce about 150 percent of the pressure to which the gun is normally subject. Guns that pass the pressure test receive stamps with various proof marks indicating the type of propellant used—black or smokeless powder—and the maximum shot charge for which the proof is valid. There are also proof houses located in Birmingham, England; Eibar, Spain; St.-Étienne, France; Gardone Val Trompia, Italy; and elsewhere.

Long gun — A generic term that loosely defines shotguns and rifles.

Low gun — The starting position for shooting Olympic-style skeet, the original version of American-style skeet, FITAS, and some other forms of sporting clays. In the low-gun position, the toe of the stock must be visible below the shooter's elbow prior to the emergence of the target. In some instances, a piece of colored tape affixed to the competitor's vest or clothing marks the shooter's elbow, and the buttstock of the shotgun must touch that tape prior to launch of the target. See **FITAS**.

Lubrication — The application of lubricant to a firearm. Apply lubricants sparingly to firearms, as an excess may drain into the head of the buttstock, causing it to soften.

Lump — The steel projections on the bottom of the barrel of single- and double-barrel shotguns that accept the locking bolt, holding the barrels tightly to the action when the gun is in battery. In forging the barrels from bar stock, lumps are now part of the process; previous to the introduction of these integral, or "chopper," lumps, gunmakers affixed lumps onto the barrels by dovetailing and brazing. In monobloc-style construction, the lumps are part of the monobloc and become integral with the barrels after insertion and soldering into the monobloc. See **battery, chopper lumps, dropper lumps, monobloc**.

Magazin (Ger.) – "Magazine."

Magazine — The portion of a firearm that holds the fresh rounds until they cycle into the chamber for firing. All repeating shotguns have magazines, most in the form of a tube that runs underneath the barrel. Bolt-action shotguns most often have box-style magazines that stack the rounds vertically; however, some bolt-action shotguns use a tubular-style magazine. Never refer to a magazine as a "clip." See **tubular magazine.**

Magazine cutoff — A device on a repeating shotgun that blocks the feeding of rounds from the magazine when the shooter opens the chamber to change rounds, check the bore for an obstruction, or change choke tubes. A small lever on the side of the receiver normally activates the cutoff. Despite its usefulness, few shotguns employ a cutoff, save the Browning Auto-5, the Gold and BPS pump, the Beretta 300 series, and the new (1999) Benelli Nova pump.

Magazine follower — The tubular cap that encapsulates the magazine spring in a tubular magazine. It is against the follower that the crimped end of the cartridge rests; the follower and magazine spring push the cartridge out of the magazine upon release of the magazine latch.

Magazine latch — A spring or spring-loaded device that holds the cartridges in the magazine until the action cycles and ejects the spent round. The magazine latch then trips, releasing the next cartridge to be fed into the chamber.

Magnum — **1.** A cartridge with a heavier than normal load, and often of longer than normal length. **2.** A shotgun whose chamber will accept extra-long cartridges.

Mainspring housing — Found on the Baker 12/20, which has an odd style of mainspring that needs to be enclosed in order to stay in position.

Manton, Joseph (1766–1835) — The father of the modern shotgun. His work led to the modern double shotgun, which has not changed significantly since about 1880.

Manual safety — A safety catch that the shooter must engage. See **automatic safety.**

Martillo (Sp.) – "Hammer."

Martini action — A single-shot rifle action that British gunmakers such as Greener adapted to the shotgun. A strong hammerless action, it employs a pivoting breechblock operated by a lever.

Matched pair — Two shotguns of the same dimensions, barrel length, weight, and so forth, that the same gunmaker manufactured separately, years or perhaps even decades apart. An individual wanting a matched pair will return to the maker a previously manufactured shotgun in order for another of identical specifications to be made. A "matched pair" is not a "true pair"—two identical guns made at the same time. See **composed pair, true pair.**

Matte finish — A dull, flat finish for either wood or metal that waterfowlers and turkey hunters favor because it helps them to conceal their guns. This style finish has the advantage of holding oil very well, owing to the large number of minute surface pores.

Matte rib — A solid, flat rib that is attached throughout its length to the barrel or barrels with the top filed to a matte finish. Winchester Repeating Arms Company used this style of rib as an extra-cost option on Model 1897, 97, 12, and 21 shotguns.

McIntosh, Michael — A former English professor and Shakespearean scholar, McIntosh is considered an authority on double shotguns. He has published several books on double guns and double-gun lore, among which is a definitive book on the A. H. Fox company. He is also a columnist for several sporting monthlies. See **p.138.**

McIntosh, Michael

Merkel — Established in 1535, Merkel, manufactured by Suhler Jagd-und Sportwaffen GmBH in Suhl, Germany, is perhaps the best known of all the German manufacturers—at least in terms of sporting shotguns. Many returning World War II veterans brought a "liberated" Merkel home with them. Recently, Merkel modernized their line of over/under shotguns by introducing a new action that uses coil springs in place of the traditional leaf or V springs, and by inverting the hammers or tumblers to achieve a better striking angle. Merkel makes a complete line of drillings, side-by-sides, over/unders, and double rifles.

Metal-to-wood fit — One of the criteria for judging the workmanship of a shotgun. In fine, handmade shotguns, the wood—buttstock and fore-end—fit so closely to the metal that the two seem to flow into each other. Wood that projects above the surface of the surrounding metal is "proud." Original Winchester Model 12 pump-action repeaters exemplify this style of fitting wood "proud of the metal."

Mid bead — A small bead on the rib, approximately halfway from breech to muzzle, for the purpose of providing better alignment of the eye and barrel. Useful to trap and skeet shooters, who premount their shotguns, the mid bead is of little use to game shooters, whose concentration is on the bird.

Midi — See **clay target**.

Mini — See **clay target**.

Misfire — Any misfire is the failure of a round to fire. There are several possible causes: a broken firing pin, a broken hammer spring, dirt clogging the mechanism, or a faulty round—one with no primer, a defective primer, defective or wet propellant, or no propellant. Gently eject any misfired round and examine it for the cause of failure; then closely examine the gun. A shotgun shell with a primer but no propellant will normally make a soft noise. The shot will clear the muzzle, but the wad almost always remains in the bore; clear it with a cleaning rod or other tool. In any case, it is crucial first to clear the firearm of all live rounds, then clear the bore of the wad, and carefully determine the cause of the misfire. A misfired round might possibly discharge within a second or two of attempting to fire it, but once ejected there is almost no chance that it will fire. In a rifle whose barrel is very hot, the round might "cook off," but there is almost no chance that this will occur in a shotgun.

Moneymaker Guncraft — A firm that installed aftermarket ventilated ribs, primarily on American-made shotguns, such as the Winchester Model 12.

Monobloc — A method of manufacturing side-by-side and over/under shotguns whereby the gunmaker forges and strikes barrel tubes, then inserts and silver-solders them into a breech section or monobloc that carries the lumps and ejector cuts. A simpler method of constructing double guns, the monobloc is easier to machine than is the process of forging barrels with integral lumps and then assembling them. In monobloc construction, the manufacturer can cold-hammer forge the barrels and virtually finish them inside and out before assembly into the monobloc. Similarly, before joining to the barrels, it is possible to cut the locking lugs and do the machining necessary for the extractors.

Monte Carlo — A style of buttstock for trapshooting that features a high, raised comb that is level for several inches, then drops off gracefully at the heel. The advantage of this stock is that it allows the shooter's head to remain upright, with the eyes level. This style of stock also compensates for shooters with long necks, and it helps ease recoil by keeping the butt in line with the barrels, allowing recoil to come straight back and be absorbed by the large muscles of the body.

Mossberg, O. F., & Sons, Inc. — The American producer of repeating shotguns. Notable in their line is the 835 UltiMag pump, which, in cooperation with Federal Cartridge Company, was the first shotgun to take the 3½-inch, 12-gauge shell. In this cooperative effort, Federal designed the load, which closely approaches the payload and ballistics of the 3½-inch, 10-bore shell, and Mossberg modified their Model 500 pump to accept the extra-long hull, and Mossberg also backbored the barrel to near 10-gauge dimensions.

Multibarrel gun — A firearm that normally incorporates both shotgun and rifle barrels. See **drilling.**

Mündung (Ger.) — "Muzzle."

National Rifle Association (NRA) — The foremost advocate of the rights of firearm owners in the United States. Membership numbers fluctuate between 2.5 and 3 million. Many rate the NRA as the most effective lobbying organization in the United States. In addition, the NRA is the regulating body for all rifle and pistol competition in the United States, and it is the national representative for all international competition, including Olympic-style skeet and trap.

National Skeet Shooting Association (NSSA) — The regulating body for skeet shooting in the United States. It endorses registered competitions, keeps members' scores and averages, and establishes rules for competition.

National Wild Turkey Federation — A U.S. conservation organization whose purpose is to further turkey hunting and turkey conservation and, on a broader scale, the maintenance and promotion of increasing areas of habitat suitable for the propagation of the wild turkey.

Needham ejectors — The first ejector system for side-by-side shotguns, developed and patented in 1874.

Night gun — A tool of market hunters, the night gun was either a large-bore or multibarrel shotgun that mounted onto the bow of a low-profile boat. A kerosene light with highly polished reflectors illuminated resting flocks of waterfowl on the water. Seemingly mesmerized by the light, the birds would bunch tightly together as the boat sculled ever closer. Once within optimum range, the gun was devastatingly effective.

Nonejector — A double shotgun, normally a boxlock, that does not have ejector springs and hammers in the fore-end but rather uses only extractors, which raise the fired hulls for manual removal. The extractor toe, a small projection on the knuckle of the action between the cocking levers, pushes the extractors upward. These guns are useful for rough shooting or walking up birds behind dogs, not for driven shooting, where speedy reloading is paramount. In the marketplace, these shotguns are often remarkably good values for those seeking a shotgun by a major maker.

Nontoxic shot — Any type of shotgun pellet that does not cause chemical poisoning to migratory waterfowl. Historically, waterfowl, especially puddle ducks such as mallards, have been susceptible to lead poisoning as a result of ingesting spent shotgun pellets lying on the bottoms of shallow ponds and potholes. Some of these ducks that sicken or die through lead poisoning then become food for predators, which in turn absorb the toxic substance. Even if the birds or animals survive the lead poisoning, either ducks or predators may fail to reproduce, or their offspring may suffer debilitating deformities and subsequently die.

Nontoxic shot: *Currently approved nontoxic shot.* **(Left to right)** *Kent tungsten/polymer; Bismuth Cartridge Company bismuth/tin shot, steel shot; and Federal Cartridge Company's tungsten/polymer shot.*

Prior to the early 1990s, the only practical nontoxic pellet was steel shot. One problem with steel shot, however, was that because it is so hard, it would damage standard shotgun barrels. Two types of damage would occur: barrel-scoring, where one or more of the hard steel pellets escape the protective plastic wad and cut into the bore; and bulging at the choke. Firing steel shot through a full-choked shotgun would cause the choke to bulge outward, forming a ring. This condition, in shotguns whose makers had designed them for lead shot, usually occurred within the first few rounds, and the bulge generally was measurable at 0.005 inch and visible to the eye. Once the bulging reached 0.005 to 0.008 inch, it usually stopped, although bulging up to .015 inch has been recorded. On double shotguns, this bulge almost always resulted in separation of the barrels.

Ballistically, soft iron is lighter than lead, and it became necessary to shoot pellets one or two sizes larger than traditional lead loads. For example, someone shooting No. 4 lead at ducks would need to shoot No. 2 steel to achieve the same approximate results. Furthermore, beyond about forty to forty-five yards, soft iron or steel loses speed too rapidly to be reliable.

In seeking approval for nontoxic shot in the United States, manufacturers must prove to the satisfaction of the U.S. Fish and Wildlife Service that the pellets will neither poison birds ingesting it nor cause birth defects in chicks. Recently, bismuth/tin and tungsten/polymer have received full or conditional approval as nontoxic shot. These softer kinds of shot do not harm shotgun barrels, and because they are heavier, they are ballistically more like lead—tungsten/polymer especially so, as the amount of tungsten can be varied.

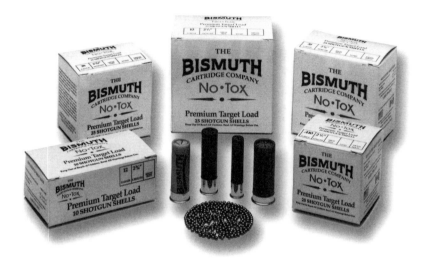

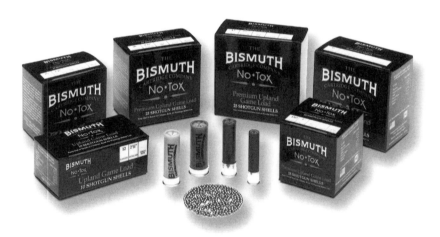

Nontoxic shotshells: *Bismuth was the first nontoxic alternative to steel shot.*

Normal, The — A semiautomatic shotgun developed and
patented by the Danish gunmaker Christian Sjörgren and

marketed in
the United Kingdom as the Normal, this
shotgun operated on the counterrecoil principle
whereby the countermotion of an inertia block following
recoil unlocked the breechbolt. Currently, Benelli uses
the counterrecoil principle to operate their series of
semiautomatic shotguns.

Notch — Also called the sear notch, the notch is the cut in the
tumbler or hammer that engages the sear. See **sear.**

9.1mm — A very small-caliber shotgun often called a "garden
gun," intended for use on pests.

Nydar sight — A sight that used a prismatic lens with rings,
much like an aerial machine-gunner's sight but reduced
in scale. War surplus and sporting goods stores sold
these sights during the early 1950s. Somewhat fragile,
and dim in all but the best of light, the Nydar sight
was never successful.

Oak and leather: *Fine gun luggage can trace its origin back to the matchlock era. The traditional oak and leather case, fitted with accessories, represents a high point in the craft. Photo courtesy of Huey Guncases of Kansas City.*

Oak and leather — The traditional hard case for best-quality shotguns. These heavy trunks are fitted to each individual shotgun as well as being fitted for all the attendant cleaning accessories, oil bottles, spare strikers, and other items.

Oberfel, Dr. George G., and Thompson, Charles E. — Authors of the 1960 book *Mysteries of Shotgun Patterns,* which delves into the statistical aspects of shotgun patterns.

Obstructions, barrel — Next only to careless handling, this is the greatest potential hazard of shotgunning. Any kind of obstruction—mud, snow, or a wad from an improperly loaded shell—creates the potential for a burst barrel. It is doubtful that a large insect would cause a bulge or burst, although an insect that has built some kind of nest in a neglected barrel might easily cause a burst or a bulge. The steel of shotgun barrels is relatively soft and very thin. Whereas a rifle barrel is thick enough to permit the placing of a single layer of plastic tape across the muzzle to keep out rain or snow, a shotgun barrel will not tolerate even that slight obstruction. Anytime an obstruction is suspected, unload the gun immediately and inspect the bore. Even partial obstructions can be highly dangerous. For removing an obstruction a cleaning rod is the most common tool, but a field expedient such as a tree branch or cornstalk will also suffice.

Off face — A condition in which the barrels of a double shotgun no longer tightly close against the standing breech face. This usually results from firing a great number of shells, or from firing shells of higher pressure or heavier load than the manufacturer recommends, or simply from the breech continually being slammed shut. In any case, if the gun warrants repair, a competent gunsmith can put it back on face, normally through building up the surface of the hook or replacing the hinge pin with one of greater diameter, or both. See **hinge pin, hook, standing breech.**

Oil bottle — A small round or square metal bottle, specifically one in an oak and leather case, that holds lubricating oil. These bottles have a small rod in the screw-off cap that enables the user to dispense only small amounts of oil from the bottle. Although it is now more of a curiosity, at one time no gun cabinet was complete without an oil bottle. See **oak and leather.**

Oil bottle: A fitted case with all accessories will contain an oil bottle like this.

Old hats — The original form of trapshooting, in which officials placed pigeons under gentlemen's top hats. At the shooter's call, an official toppled the hat by pulling a string attached to the hat so the pigeon could fly free.

Olin, John — One of the significant names in American shotgun lore. Olin was the innovator behind the modern magnum shotshell, as well as one of the saviors of the Winchester Repeating Arms Company; his father, Franklin, had bought the company at a receiver's sale, and John Olin ran it following his father's death. John Olin was the moving force behind the development of the Winchester Model 21 side-by-side, and he also recognized the need for hunters and the shooting industry to become involved in conservation.

Olin/Winchester — The present-day ammunition-manufacturing company that is a part of Olin Industries, a diversified company. They chose the name Olin/Winchester in an effort to define the company, and to resolve confusion between themselves as an ammunition company and the U.S. Repeating Arms Company, which manufactures sporting arms and which uses the trademarked name Winchester under license from Olin/Winchester.

Olympic skeet — The version of skeet at the Olympic Games and at other international competitions, such as the Pan American Games. In this style of skeet, the competitor must dismount his gun from the shoulder, so that a portion of the butt is visible beneath the elbow until the target emerges from the trap house. In addition, there is a varying sequence of target releases, from instantaneous to a delay of up to three seconds. In terms of the targets shot, stations one and seven are doubles only (the simultaneous release of two targets, one from each house); on stations two, three, five, and six, both singles and doubles are shot, and single targets are shot on station four. See **skeet**.

Olympic trap — The style of trap in international competitions such as the Olympic Games and the Pan American Games. It is similar to down-the-line or American-style trap, except that the traps are in a trench that runs parallel to the shooting stations. Also, there are three traps in front of each shooting position, and the speed of the targets is considerably greater than that of regular trap competitions. Each of the three traps at each shooting position is set to a different angle and height. When the competitor calls for a target, it appears from one of the three traps; the shooter does not know which trap will be released, because a computer regulates the sequence and mixes the traps. Unlike regular trap, in Olympic trap a voice-activated relay releases the targets, so there cannot be any suspicion of fast or slow pulls.

Each competitor may take two shots per target, and shooters move to the next position following each shot. Because the squad is always in motion, a sixth shooter is part of the squad, although there are only five shooting positions. The extra shooter ensures that the squad is always ready to shoot without having to wait for a shooter to reposition himself.

O

On face — A double shotgun whose breech is tight and whose barrels properly close against the standing-breech face.

Oval — An oval-shaped inlay in the belly of a shotgun stock upon which the owner may have his initials engraved. Save for bespoke shotguns, few ovals ever receive such engraving.

Oval: A small metal plate in the stock that can be engraved with the owner's initials, though most are not.

Overboring — The process of boring a shotgun barrel to larger than standard diameter. See **backboring.**

Over/under — The most common name for a double-barrel shotgun whose barrels are arranged one atop the other. By far the most popular style of shotgun during the last twenty-five years of the twentieth century, the over/under combines the single sighting plane of the repeater with some of the handling qualities and balance of a side-by-side. Because of the stiffness of the over/under's barrels, these shotguns also tend to shoot more consistently at or above the point of aim; side-by-side barrels tend to flex downward more upon firing, owing to the less stiff barrels.

P

Pachmayr, August — The Los Angeles gunsmith most famous for his recoil pads. In addition to producing Pachmayr pads, his firm also did fine custom gunsmithing on both rifles and shotguns. For a complete biography, see *Frank A. Pachmayr: America's Master Gunsmith* by John Lachuk (1995 Safari Press).

Pair — 1. Two shotguns, either precisely matched or closely matched in terms of weight, barrel length, stock dimensions, etc. See **composed pair, composite pair, matched pair, true pair.** 2. Two game birds—that is, a pair of ducks, geese, etc. See **company terms.** 3. In skeet, trap, or sporting clays, two clay targets at which the shooter must fire two shots without reloading. See **following pair, report pair, simultaneous pair, skeet, sporting clays.**

Pan — The part of the lock of a flintlock firearm that holds very finely granulated powder. When the flint, which is on the hammer, strikes the frizzen, a shower of sparks ignites this fine powder. The resulting flame travels through a small connecting hole into the bore, where it touches off the main powder charge. See **flintlock, frizzen.**

Pape, William Rochester — Although American folklore widely credits the Illinois market hunter Fred Kimble with the invention of choke boring for shotgun barrels, the truth is that the first U.S. patent covering choke boring went to the American gunsmith Sylvester Roper on 10 April 1866, beating out the British gunsmith William Pape of Newcastle, England, by about six weeks. However, in an era of slow communication, Pape's discovery is significant, and the fact that only six weeks' interval separated the two inventors means that Pape and Roper experienced the phenomenon we today call parallel development. However, J. W. Long, in his book *American Wildfowling,* states that Jeremiah Smith of Southfield, Rhode Island, invented choke boring in 1827, predating both Pape and Roper by nearly forty years. See **Kimble, Roper, Smith.**

Paradox gun — A shotgun whose bore is for the most part smooth but has rifling in the last few inches (normally, the last two). In theory, this gun is capable of firing either shot or a slug; the ball or bullet engages sufficient rifling to provide the spin necessary for accurate shooting. Intended to displace multibarrel guns such as drillings, paradox guns seem to have been effective as big-game rifles, providing the user with the handling qualities of a shotgun. Although the popularity of these guns waned following World War I, firms such as Holland & Holland continued to catalog and manufacture them until the 1950s.

Parallels — In bored chokes, the parallel section between the beginning of the actual choke constriction and the muzzle. This style of choking is most common in best-quality shotguns, but it was also a design feature in pre-1964 Winchester Model 12 pump-action and Model 21 side-by-side shotguns. The design employs a gradual taper into the choke constriction; the parallels then maintain that constriction to the muzzle.

Parallèles (Fr.) — "Double-barrel shotgun."

Paralelli (Ital.) — "Double-barrel shotgun."

Parker Brothers — Located in Meriden, Connecticut, Parker shotguns were and still are one of America's premier side-by-side shotguns. Charles Parker began producing the shotguns that bore his name in 1866. Made in exposed-hammer and hammerless models in every gauge, the Parker shotgun was one of the most popular and most highly regarded double guns of its day. Of the American doubles, the Parker is the most sought-after and most collected shotgun of its type. Some of the Parker's most endearing qualities were shotguns manufactured on true-size frames, so that a 12-gauge magnum did not have a frame the same size as the light, upland-intended 12. The 28-gauge also had its own frame, as did the diminutive .410-bore. The customer could select from light, standard, and heavy frames, as well as many other options. As with virtually every other American manufacturer of side-by-sides, the twentieth century was not kind to Parker. In 1934 Remington Arms Company purchased Parker, and for all intents and purposes the last Parker left the Remington factory around 1947. In the 1980s, a series called Parker Reproductions was manufactured to exact Parker specifications in Japan. The parts from these shotguns would fully interchange with original Parker parts, and they were stocked in highly figured wood. Selling for collector's prices approaching that of the original Parker, the last of the reproductions was sold in the mid-1990s. Thought by many to be a handmade shotgun, the Parker was certainly a hand-assembled shotgun, but was made in the manner of the typical American assembly line. Parker shotguns were not handmade by British standards but were extremely well finished. The Parker was a reliable shotgun, and many are still being shot at the beginning of the twenty-first century.

Parkerizing — An extremely durable finish that converts the metal surface to a thin layer of crystalline iron phosphate, sometimes called a phosphate finish. Manufacturers applied it mainly to military small arms. The matte finish it produces holds oil and rust inhibitors very well, and, because of its black-to-greenish color, it is an excellent camouflage. Although popular in the 1980s with waterfowl and turkey hunters, it has now given way to more modern dipped camouflage finishes. See **dipped finish.**

Parsons, Herb — (1913-1963) Born in Tennessee, Herb Parsons grew up hunting and shooting; he also played minor league baseball. For a number of years he was the premier exhibition shooter for Winchester Repeating Arms. His show-closing stunt was to throw seven clay targets into the air and break them all, using a

Winchester Model 12 pump-action shotgun, before any hit the ground. Other tricks included shooting through the center of washers with a rifle, and throwing clay targets between his legs, then picking up a shotgun and breaking them before any touched the ground. Parsons won the 1950 and 1951 World's Duck Calling Championship, and he always included a duck-calling demonstration in his shooting exhibitions. At one time he sold duck calls at these events that were made for him in Stuttgart, Arkansas, by the late D. M. "Chick" Major. Parsons suffered from heart problems and died in 1963 at age fifty.

Herb Parsons: *Winchester's premier exhibition shooter and world duck-calling champion.*

Partridge – A term that is both specific to a family of game birds and is used colloquially to describe upland birds that are not members of the partridge family, such as the ruffed grouse. The most common partridges are the Spanish red-legged (often called a chukar), the Hungarian, and, in South America, the perdiz, which is smaller than the other two. These birds are larger than the various quail but only two-thirds the size of a Chinese ringneck pheasant. As a game bird, especially when they are wild birds, partridge provide excellent sport and are equally good as table fare.

Patrone (Ger.) – "Cartridge."

Patronenlager (Ger.) – "Chamber."

Pattern — The dispersion of the shot charge. Once the shot leaves the muzzle it spreads to varying degrees, and the manner in which it spreads is the shotgun's pattern. Many shotgunners test their guns at a patterning board, using either preprinted shotgun patterning targets or large sheets of plain brown or white paper. The results give an indication as to what the average spread and distribution of the pellets will be from shot to shot when using the same brand, load, and lot of shells. The industry standard is to shoot at a target at a measured 40 yards, then enclose the largest number of pellets within a 30-inch circle, count them, and determine the percentage of pellets from the entire load that are within the circle.

Many factors affect patterns, chiefly the choke constriction. However, shotgun barrels of the same make and configuration can produce widely differing patterns. Patterns vary according to bore diameter, forcing cone configuration, choke style and constriction, shot size, and shot weight and velocity. With the nearly universal use of screw-in choke tubes, it is far easier to regulate patterns, as constriction can change by as little as 0.005 inch between tubes; a great diversity of patterns can result from switching tubes.

Most bespoke shotguns still use fixed chokes; a highly experienced barrel borer regulates them to a specific shot size, weight, and velocity. In pattern testing, it is tempting to shoot one pattern and take that as representative. In fact, three to five patterns give only a general idea, and one hundred provide only an indication of what that particular gun/choke/ammunition combination will yield.

Standard pattern percentages at 40 yards

Full choke	60% to 70%
Modified choke	55% to 60%
Improved cylinder	45%

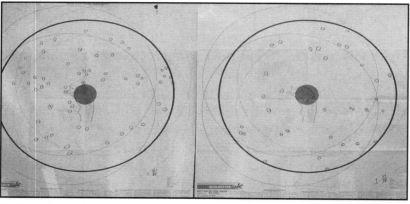

Patterning: An example of two pattern sheets showing the hits from two shots. Sheets such as this are used to evaluate the performance of combinations of barrel/ammunition and chokes to achieve optimum performance from a particular shotgun.

Patterning is also useful in gun fitting. Here, however, one disregards the patterning efficiency of the barrel/ammunition in favor of plotting where the shot charge strikes in relation to a premarked aiming point. The shooter concentrates on the marked aiming point, shoulders the shotgun, and quickly fires. Based on the patterns fired, an experienced fitter can then determine

P

the proper stock dimensions for that particular shooter. One technique for verifying fit or to see if changes to the stock are necessary is to shoot at the pattern board from exactly 16 yards; a trend should emerge from the patterns. Measuring from the center of the aiming point, each inch of displacement of the pattern translates to a stock adjustment of 1/16 inch. See **backboring, bore, choke, gun fit, overboring, screw-in chokes.**

Pattern board — A simple frame onto which a large sheet of paper can be clamped or stapled for the purpose of establishing gun fit or choke/ammunition performance. At one time, patterning was done against a whitewashed steel or iron plate. The pellets hitting the white surface made dark spots and then they were counted. Because of the danger of ricochet and because it is easier to count patterns and record data away from the range, the use of paper pattern sheets has become universal.

Patterning — The act of pattern-testing a shotgun.

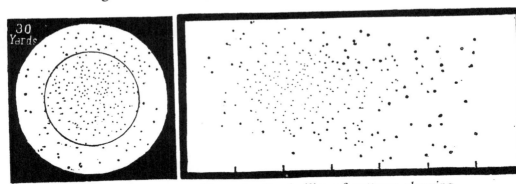

Patterning: *Cylinder at 30 yards. Facsimiles of patterns showing both lateral deviation and stringing of the same pellets.*

Pattern plate — A plate of steel or iron with a coating of white paint or whitewash and a reference or aiming spot. Hits by lead shot leave behind splashes of lead on the white background, showing the shot pattern. Because of the danger of ricochets, especially with steel shot, pattern plates are no longer in use.

Pear drop – A style of drop point. The pear drop is larger than normal and serves as a transitional area between the action and the wrist of the stock. See **drop point.**

Pellet — The most common projectile for use in shotguns; collectively, the usual term for pellets is "shot." Manufacturers produce pellets of lead/antimony, soft iron or steel, tungsten/iron, tungsten/polymer, bismuth/tin, and pure tin. Pellets come in varying sizes, from dust through very large buckshot. Common American sizes run from 000 to No. 4 buckshot and finer shot from BB through No. 9, although at one time the Federal Cartridge Company loaded No. 10 shot for the U.S. Army Skeet Team.

Pellet size — American lead pellets run from 000 buckshot through No. 12 shot. The most common sizes are Nos. 2, 4, 5, 6, 7½, 8, and 9; although soft iron or steel shot is lighter than lead shot, they conform to the same standard diameters. Following are the inch and millimeter sizes of currently produced pellets:

Buckshot

Shot size	000	00	0	No. 1	No. 2	No. 3	No. 4
Inch	0.36	0.33	0.32	0.30	0.27	0.25	0.24
Millimeters	9.14	8.38	8.13	7.62	6.86	6.35	6.10

Lead Shot

Shot size	BB	2	4	5	6	7 ½	8	8 ½	9	12
Inch	0.180	0.150	0.130	0.120	0.110	0.095	0.090	0.085	0.080	0.05
Millimeters	4.57	3.81	3.30	3.05	2.79	2.41	2.29	2.16	2.03	1.27

Steel Shot

Shot size	F	T	BBB	BB	Air Rifle	1	2	3	4	5	6
Inch	0.22	0.20	0.19	0.18	0.17	0.16	0.15	0.14	0.13	0.12	0.11
Millimeters	5.59	5.08	4.83	4.57	4.49	4.06	3.81	3.56	3.30	3.05	2.79

Perazzi — Manufactured in Brescia, Italy, since 1952, the Perazzi has become one of the world's leading competitive shotguns, and the choice of many competitive skeet, trap, and live bird shooters. In addition, Perazzi manufactures stylish game guns in a great variety of gauges and styles.

Percussion cap — A small, cup-shaped cap that is fitted over the nipple of a percussion-lock firearm. This cap contained fulminate of mercury or other volatile compound that, when struck by the hammer, directs a hot, brilliant jet of flame through the hollow nipple, into the barrel, and directly into the powder charge, igniting it and firing the gun. The percussion cap was a major step forward from the loose powder priming of the flintlock. It was far less susceptible to moisture, far safer, and far more reliable.

   During the firing of a flintlock shotgun, the priming charge burned directly beside the shooter's face, often resulting in a burn or even blinding the shooter. Although the percussion cap was not foolproof, upon firing, the hammer essentially covered the cap, and there was far less likelihood of the propellant gases escaping toward the shooter. Succeeded directly by the pinfire, the percussion cap was the precursor to the modern primer. See **pinfire primer.**

Percussion lock — The style of ignition system of the mid- to late nineteenth century, and the main precursor to the modern breechloading shotgun. In this system, the shooter loaded powder, wad, shot and overshot wad from the muzzle, then placed a percussion cap over the nipple. When the hammer dropped, it crushed the percussion cap, releasing a hot jet of flame into the barrel, igniting the powder charge.

Percussore (Ital.) — "Firing pin."

Percuteur (Fr.) — "Firing pin."

Percutor (Sp.) – "Firing pin."

Pheasant load — Any shotshell appropriate for shooting pheasants. Americans tend to shoot a heavier load than do Europeans. This is partly due to the running ability of pheasants and their tendency to flush well in front of the guns. In America, 12-gauge pheasant loads are normally 1¼ ounces of No. 4 or No. 6 shot, although some advocate heavy, magnum loads of 1½ ounces of No. 4. Under certain circumstances these heavy loads may be more effective, but, in the main, the normal "high brass" 12-gauge load is reliable. Twenty-gauge enthusiasts will favor one-ounce loads of No. 6 or No. 7½, and those using the 28-gauge on released birds find that ¾ ounce of No. 6 or No. 7½ shot works well on close-flushing birds.

In Europe, hunters shoot pheasants either by driving them over the guns or by walking them up, as is the case in America. While high pheasants receive much attention, many hunters shoot driven pheasant at relatively close range, 30 to 45 yards, and, because they often present their more vulnerable underside, hunters can bag them with a relatively modest load of 1, 1¹/₁₆ or 1 ¹/₈ ounce of No. 6 shot. Those who rough shoot or walk up their pheasants behind dogs find that the same loads work equally well.

Pheasants Forever — An American conservation-oriented organization that encourages cooperation between farmers and hunters and seeks to preserve the type of upland cover that promotes the reproduction and growth of upland game birds.

Pigeon gun — A shotgun solely for competitive shooting of pigeons and capable of firing two shots. Many experienced pigeon shots use the same gun for shooting American trap doubles. A pigeon gun should be relatively heavy. The extra weight helps diminish recoil, an important consideration over the course of a long competition. For choke, pigeon shooters use nothing more open than modified, with some preferring the combination of modified for the first shot and full for the second. Others prefer tighter chokes and therefore shoot improved modified for their first shot and follow up with extra-full choke for the second.

Many European shooters still favor exposed hammer guns for a perceived added measure of reliability. However, in the main, pigeon shooters shoot over/unders and occasionally semiautomatics. The semiautomatic provides more comfort from recoil; that comes, however, at the expense of having only one choke. At one time, pigeon shooters favored shotguns that delivered the first shot a bit high and the second a bit low. Point of impact is a matter of personal preference, but today many live pigeon shooters prefer the point of impact for both barrels to be just a bit high, the idea being to keep the bird always visible and never below the sighting plane. Some pigeon guns have no safety mechanisms at all.

Pigeon shooting — In parts of the United States, Mexico, and Europe, a form of trapshooting that uses live pigeons. The most difficult of the competitive shotgun sports, live pigeon shoots draw some of the greatest shots in the world to compete for big money prizes and often to participate in the betting—on both shooter and pigeon alike. See **box birds**, *colombarie.*

Pinfire — The best-known ignition systems in the transition from muzzleloading, percussion-ignition shotguns to modern self-contained shells for breechloading shotguns. The pinfire cartridge was a metal hull similar to a modern shotshell, into which was loaded powder, wads, shot, and the priming. The firing pin was a vertical, strawlike projection at the rear of the case. This projection rested on the percussion cap. Upon being struck with the hammer, it fired the cap which was in the powder charge, firing the gun.

Pins (Brit.) — Machine screws for use in the assembly of a firearm.

Pit — A type of blind or hide, almost exclusively for use in goose hunting. Pits can be several feet deep and long enough to accommodate four to six hunters. Covering the pit with cornstalks or other vegetation makes the hunters invisible to circling geese until the hunters rise to shoot.

Pitch — The measurement of the angle of the butt of a shotgun stock. Pitch governs how the butt lies on the shoulder. A shotgun with too little pitch will allow the toe of the stock to dig into the shoulder, which can lead to bruising; in addition, a shotgun with too little pitch will slide down and off the shoulder when fired. If there is too much pitch, the stock will slip up into the cheek and potentially cause painful bruising there. Careful gun fitting includes studying the shape of the individual's shoulder and chest and adjusting the pitch to keep the shotgun comfortably in position. In general, women require more pitch than men.

The most common way of measuring pitch is by standing the butt on the floor with the action or receiver against a squared door frame, then measuring the distance (or amount of pitch) from the top of the rib or barrel to the vertical doorjamb. This measurement is in inches of positive or negative pitch. Common, off-the-rack shotguns have pitch somewhere around 1½ to 4 inches, depending upon barrel length. The longer the barrel, the wider the arc, hence the larger the gap. Pitch can also be expressed as the angle of the muzzle from a right angle upon which one leg rests against the butt of the shotgun and the other leg contacts the top of the receiver or breech. For example, if one stood a shotgun with its butt on the floor with the receiver or action touching a wall that was 90 degrees to the floor, the resulting measurement of the distance of the muzzle away from the wall would be the measurement of pitch down. If the muzzle, and hence the barrel and breech, are flush with the wall, this would be called neutral pitch. If the muzzle touches the wall with the butt squarely on the floor and the receiver or action not touching, this would be called negative pitch, which is very difficult to accurately measure.

The British prefer to express pitch as a part of the measurements of the length of pull of the stock. In fitting a shotgun for pitch, which allows the butt to properly fit the individual shooter's shoulder, British gun fitters take measurements from the trigger to the toe, center, and heel of the stock, providing precise measurements for the stocker to properly adjust the pitch.

Pitting — The result of rust or corrosion on steel, pitting is especially prevalent in barrels that predate the advent of noncorrosive priming mixtures. In such barrels, heavy pitting that looks like miniature craters occurs. A pitted firearm normally loses a great deal of its resale value, although in all but the most severe cases, pitting does little to affect performance. Only when pitting is so deep as to compromise safety does it become an issue.

In refinishing a pitted gun, the gunsmith or polisher must remove the adjoining metal down to the level of the pitting. That means removing barrel metal, and, on the exterior, often the lettering of the maker's name. Unless there is a compelling reason to refinish a pitted gun, it is best to leave it as is; clean it carefully, however, so as to ensure that the pitting gets no worse.

Placa lado (Sp.) – "Side plate."

Placca lato (Ital.) – "Side plate."

Place finder (Brit.) — A small numbered strip of metal or ivory strip that a shooter draws from a cup or leather holder to determine position or butt number for a drive. It is one of the bits of ephemera that surround formal driven shooting.

Plaque laterale (Fr.) – "Side plate."

Plaquette (Fr.) – "Grip."

Plate — **1.** A term for patterning of a shotgun using a patterning board or plate. **2.** The application of an exterior metal finish by means of electroplating. For example, gunmakers use electroplating to apply the chrome lining to some shotgun bores.

Plomb disco (Fr.) — Rather than the common round shot, this shot is in the form of flattened discs of lead that, like cubed shot *(dispersante)*, spread the pattern very quickly once the shot charge leaves the barrel. It is useful in tightly choked barrels when open patterns are desirable. See *dispersante,* **spreader wad.**

Plug — A device—normally a plastic, metal, or wooden rod— the hunter inserts into the tubular magazine of a pump-action or semiautomatic shotgun to reduce the magazine's capacity. In the United States and Canada, it is unlawful to hunt migratory birds (that is, waterfowl) with a shotgun capable of firing more than three shots. Most states and provinces require that shotguns be limited to three shots regardless of the game being hunted.

Point of impact — The point at which the bulk of the shot charge strikes the target. Most current shotguns center their shot charge a bit high, on the order of 4 to 8 inches above the line of sight at 40 yards. Trapshooting guns print their patterns 6 to 12 inches high at 40 yards. Because of their more flexible barrels, side-by-sides often throw their patterns a bit low. For example, through the 1960s, Winchester regulated their Model 21 to shoot slightly low. In 1960, they determined that 21s should shoot dead on and made the necessary change. Over/unders, because one barrel sits atop the other, are much stiffer than the barrels of a side-by-side; they often shoot higher because of their greatly reduced flex.

Polvoro (Sp.) — "Powder," or "propellant."

Poly Choke — Perhaps the most popular of variable choking devices that predate the screw-in choke. E. Field White developed this device for use on pump and semiautomatic shotguns. It was a series of flexible fingers that the shooter can compress or relax by adjusting a surrounding collet. The tapered collet, when tightened, causes the fingers to draw inward, increasing the constriction.

Poly Choke advertised that their device produced "nine degrees of choke" between the most open "slug" setting and extra full. These devices, and others like them (such as Herter's Vari-Choke), do provide some change in pattern density, but not as much as their advertising would have had one believe. Today you are most likely

Poly Choke: *One of the various styles of variable choke that were popular during the first two-thirds of the twentieth century. Still manufactured by Marble Arms, these chokes have been largely superseded by screw-in chokes.*

to see this collet-style choke on used guns, although Marble Arms is still producing the Poly Choke.

Pompa (Sp.) – "Pump action."

Pompa (Ital.) – "Pump action."

Pompe (Fr.) – "Pump action."

Port — **1.** The cut in the side or bottom of the receiver of a pump-action or semiautomatic shotgun through which the fired hull ejects. **2.** The hole or holes in the bottom of the barrel of a semiautomatic shotgun through which the propellant gas travels to the piston, initiating the cycling of the action.

Porting — The cutting of small holes at the muzzle end of a shotgun barrel immediately behind the choke area, to vent the propellant gases upward. Porting attenuates recoil and improves pattern performance. Shotguns with ported barrels display very little muzzle rise or jump, permitting the shooter to have continuous visual contact with the target and removing most or all of the upward recoil against the face.

Posten (Ger.) — "Buckshot."

Poudre (Fr.) — "Powder," or "propellant."

Powder — The common term for propellant. Modern shotgun powders are progressive-burning propellants that burn at a controlled rate; normally, all the powder has burned by the time the shot charge exits the muzzle. Before the invention of smokeless powder, guns fired black powder. Although black powder generates pressures that are quite low, the powder explodes rather than burns. Smokeless powder does not explode; it burns at a predictable rate, but reaches much higher pressures than black powder.

The rate of burn is important in keeping loads within permissible pressures, and manufacturers formulate shotgun powders for specific applications. Fast-burning powders, such as Red Dot and Clays, are for target loads; they have a fast pressure peak to move the relatively light shot charge. Magnum loads use slow-burning powders such as Blue Dot that very gradually achieve peak pressure; they push the heavy charge of shot up the barrel more slowly at first, rising to peak pressure once more space is available, thereby keeping the pressures at safe levels. See **propellant.**

Powell, William & Son, Ltd. — Established in Birmingham, England, in 1802, Powell still produces a limited number of side-by-side shotguns each year.

Powell, William & Son, Ltd.: *A perfect miniature flintlock, made by Wiliam Powell in 1830 and measuring 8¾ inches.*

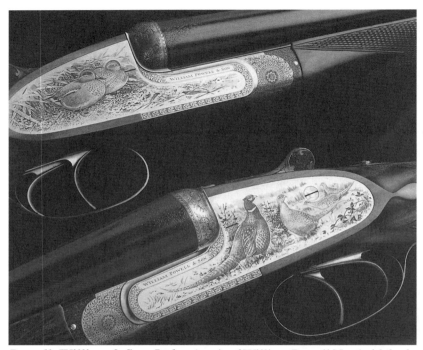

Powell, William & Son, Ltd.: *A pair of William Powell No. 1 sidelocks with specially commissioned game scene engraving.*

Pressure — All firearms are subject to the forces of the expanding gases that form as a result of the burning of the propellant; collectively, these forces constitute pressure. Manufacturers design and proof firearms to be able to withstand the normal, prescribed pressures for the length of cartridge and the specified shot load. If pressures rise too high, it is possible to burst the barrel, although more subtle damage normally occurs, in the form of loosening of the action. Shooters using factory-loaded ammunition of the appropriate length and load should have no reason to worry. However, those who handload need to pay strict attention to loading data and ensure that their loading equipment drops the exact amount of propellant and shot. When handloading, use only the components specified in the data. See **handloading, proofing, SAAMI, service pressure.**

Pressure gun — A carriage supporting heavy barrels of specific caliber or gauge, the pressure gun can definitively establish the pressure that specific loads create. Today, manufacturers routinely and frequently test their ammunition using a pressure gun. Large operations such as Olin/Winchester, Remington, and Federal Cartridge run random test batches of ammunition through their pressure guns every few minutes during production to ensure uniformity.

Early pressure guns used a lead or copper crusher within a piston that entered the chamber and rested against the cartridge. Upon firing, the piston compressed the crusher. By measuring the length of the crusher and comparing that measurement with its initial length, it was possible to establish a pressure reading. Such readings appeared as Lead Units of Pressure (LUP) or Copper Units of Pressure (CUP). In recent years piezoelectric transducers have replaced copper and lead crushers; they provide direct readings in pounds per square inch. Data derived from pressure gun testing ensures uniformity and safety.

Pressure gun: *This pressure gun owned by Hodgdon Powders and used in their laboratory in Shawnee Mission, Kansas, can accurately measure the pressure generated by a particular cartridge. It is used by all ammunition and component manufacturers to test loaded ammunition to ensure that it meets all requirements of safe pressure and velocity. This particular pressure gun is fired with compressed air so that each strike of the primer is uniform.*

Primer — The ignition source for all current cartridges. The primer in shotshells is called a battery-cup or Boxer primer in honor of its inventor, Col. Edward Munier Boxer, who thought of putting the anvil within the primer itself. The outside of the primer is a steel cup that contains the encapsulated priming mixture; at the end closest to the propellant is an anvil. Upon firing, the firing pin or striker and the self-contained anvil crush the priming mixture between them, causing a jet of extremely hot flame to exit through the hole located just beyond the anvil and travel into the propellant or powder charge. A sealant blocks the connecting hole between propellant and primer, preventing fine-grained propellants from migrating into the primer, causing misfires and incomplete ignition of the propellant charge.

One of the earliest problems with primers was that, while they were very reliable, the fulminate of mercury or potassium chlorate compound they used turned to a salt when fired, thereby attracting moisture and causing barrel pitting. Virtually every shotgun in use before the introduction of noncorrosive primers shows barrel pitting. Noncorrosive primers use lead styphnate, which is reliable and does not cause corrosion problems. However, with the ever-growing fear of lead compounds in the environment, its continued use may be in question. Currently, ammunition companies are seeking alternatives.

Prince of Wales grip — Similar to the half-pistol grip, this grip is midway between the standard British straight-gripped stock and the American pistol-grip stock. The true Prince of Wales is more like the straight grip, however, with only a slight amount of bend. Formed with a ball at its termination, it is a very elegant grip. While it is neither fish nor fowl, it does combine some of the strongest features of both grips. Because it is still close to the straight grip, one's hand is more in line with the barrels than is the case with the full pistol grip. On the other hand, the Prince of Wales grip provides some of the control available from the full pistol grip. Now common on shotguns for both target work and hunting, its greatest attractions are the elegant lines and the pistol-grip feel.

Proof house — In European countries, government proofing of all firearms must take place prior to sale. Proof houses first inspect firearms for safety, rejecting any that are not in compliance with set standards. Then inspectors test fire the guns under controlled conditions, using purposeful overloads to ensure safety and integrity.

The most notable proof house is the London Proof House, established in 1637; the Birmingham (England) Proof House followed in 1813. There are other proof houses in the major firearm-producing areas of the Continent, including St.-Etiénne in France, perhaps the oldest house in existence; Eibar, in the Basque region of Spain; Liège, Belgium; and Gardone Val Trompia, Italy.

Proof load — A special cartridge that subjects the firearm undergoing testing to an intentional overload. Generally, proof loads generate pressures 50 percent greater than that generated by a normal cartridge specific to the arm being tested. These cartridges are a key part of proof testing and ensure that the arm will perform in a safe manner provided proper ammunition is used. Although not necessarily blue in appearance, the slang term for them is "blue pill," and these rounds are clearly marked "Danger—Proof Load." Their manufacture and distribution is very carefully regulated by the various ammunition manufacturers. The Sporting Arms and Ammunition Manufacturing Institute (SAAMI) and the International Proof Commission (C.P.I.) establish various parameters to which all ammunition and arms manufacturers subscribe. For example, SAAMI standards dictate that a 2¾-inch, 12-gauge shell have a maximum service pressure of 11,500 pounds per square inch (psi), as measured by a piezoelectric transducer mounted in a pressure gun. Therefore the proof-test pressure is in the neighborhood of 17,250 psi. Ammunition manufacturers will not release data regarding the pressures of their proof loads. See **blue pill, service pressure.**

Proof marks — The various markings by national governments— or, in the case of American manufacturers, individual manufacturers—to indicate that the firearms upon which they appear have been proof tested and are safe for use with the recommended shells or cartridges.

Proof marks: *The action (background) carries Spanish proof marks from the Eibar Proof House. The barrels in the foreground have British proof marks from the Birmingham Proof House.*

Italian Proofmarks

Distinctive mark
of the Gardone
proofhouse
applies to all arms

Additional mark
for arms proved
in a finished state

Definitive
blackpowder
proof PN

Definitive
smokeless
proof PSF

Discretionary
superior
smokeless proof PSF

West German Proofmarks

Definitive
blackpowder
proof *SP*

Definitive
smokeless
proof *N*

Superior
smokeless
proof *V*

Reproof *J*

Distinctive marks of various proofhouses

Ulm   Berlin   Kiel   Hanover   Munich Mellrichstadt Cologne

British Proofmarks

	LONDON	BIRMINGHAM
Provisional barrel proof		

		LONDON	BIRMINGHAM
Definitive smokeless proof			
	On action	On barrel	

Definitive blackpowder proof		

Special definitive proof		

Reproof		

Belgian Proofmarks

Muzzleloading shotguns and smoothbores

Normal   Superior

Barrel   Lock   Barrel   Lock

Breechloading shotguns

Discretionary   Normal   Superior
provisional   Required proof
barrel proof   Barrel and action parts

Smallbore rifles   Smokeless proof

 Blackpowder
proof

Barrel
Barrel   Action parts   Action parts

Rifled arms

 Required
proof
Barrel
Action parts

Austrian Proofmarks

VIENNA   FERLACH   VIENNA   FERLACH

Provisional barrel proof   Definitive smokeless proof

Definitive blackpowder proof   Discretionary superior proof
for shotguns

Spanish Proofmarks

Eibar proofmark
applied to all arms   Blackpowder proof
for muzzleloaders

Voluntary
blackpowder proof for   Required
breechloader barrels   smokeless proof
for breechloading
smoothbores

Supplementary
smokeless proof   Proof
for breechloading   for smallbore
smoothbores   pistols and rifles

Required proof   Proof for foreign
for rifled arms   arms not carrying
the CIP mark

French Proofmarks

Required proofs

Normal proof for finished blackpowder arms

Supplementary proof for finished arms

Normal proof for finished smokeless arms

Blackpowder reproof

Superior proof for finished smokeless arms

Proof for rifled foreign long arms

Proof for rifled French long arms S‡E TIENNE

Proof for French short arms S‡E TIENNE

Proof for foreign short arms

Superior reproof

East German Proofmarks

Normal proof   Superior proof   Repair proof

Date of proof (month and year)   **474**

Proofing — 1. The act of submitting a firearm to proof. 2. The firing of a prescribed overload to ensure the safety and integrity of a firearm prior to sale.

Propellant — The proper name for smokeless powder. See **powder.**

Propellante (Ital.) – "Powder," or "propellant."

Proving — The act of proofing a firearm.

Pull — 1. One of the vital dimensions of a shotgun stock, it indicates the distance from the front trigger of a double-trigger gun (or from a single trigger) to the center of the buttstock. This dimension is commonly 14 to 14 3/8 inches in mass-produced shotguns, but in a bespoke shotgun it will depend upon the build of the shooter. British gun fitters will measure lengths of pull not only from the center of the stock but also at the heel and toe, thereby providing the most reliable determination of pitch. See **pitch.** 2. The most common command for requesting a clay target. The command "pull" goes back into the earliest history of moving-target shooting, when the trapper actually pulled a cord to release a pigeon. In later times, traps were operated by means of a long, buried rod. The trapper pushed a lever to cock the trap, pulling the lever to release the cocked trap on the command "pull" from the shooter.

Pulver (Ger.) – "Powder," or "propellant."

Pump action — One of the earliest and still the most popular style of repeating shotgun. This gun has a single barrel with a tubular magazine underneath. The action operates by pulling the fore-end rearward. At the end of the stroke, the shooter pushes the fore-end forward until the breechbolt locks into battery with either the receiver or barrel extension. The pump action is the most reliable of the repeating shotguns, since it operates manually and is not dependent upon the forces of recoil or propellant gases. Because of its manual operation the pump-action shotgun will take any shotshell of proper gauge and length, making the pump action the most versatile of repeating shotguns. Classic pump actions include the Winchester Models 1897, 97 (both with exposed hammers), and 12; Remington Models 31 and 870; the bottom-ejecting Ithaca Model 37; the Browning BPS series; and the Remington Model 17, which is similar to the Ithaca 37. See **barrel extension, battery, breechbolt, receiver, tubular magazine.**

Pump action: *The evolution of the pump-action shotgun.* **(Top to bottom)** *The exposed-hammer Winchester Model 1897, the first truly successful pump-action shotgun; the Winchester Model 12, the first hammerless pump; and the Browning BPS, representing the bottom-ejecting style of pump action.*

Pump action: *The pump-action shotgun is one of the most versatile for the waterfowl and upland bird hunter.* ***(Left to right)*** *The Browning bottom-ejecting 10-gauge BPS; a 12-gauge Winchester Model 12; another BPS in 28-gauge.*

Punt gun — A single-barrel shotgun with a very large bore, the punt gun normally fired nails, rocks, and sometimes lead shot. Hunters mounted them on low-profile boats or skiffs and used them to decimate large flocks of waterfowl resting on the water. Illegal in North America as of the beginning of the twentieth century, these guns are still in use in Great Britain and parts of Europe.

Punt gun: *Rigged to a low-profile skiff that the hunter sculled into position near a flock of resting ducks or geese, these very large-bore shotguns were capable of killing dozens of birds with a single shot. Hunters used these mainly at night, when waterfowl are most vulnerable. They became illegal during the early decades of the twentieth century. This gun and skiff are on display in the Upper Bay Museum in North East, Maryland.*

Purbaugh, Claude — A California gunsmith credited with the development of the full-length, small-gauge insert tube for twin-tube shotguns. Although Browning offered its Super Tubes—short 20- and 28-gauge and .410-bore adapters— it was Purbaugh who developed the far better full-length tube. He also converted the 20-gauge Remington 1100 semiautomatic shotgun to .28 and .410 gauges, by means of a full-length tube, an altered breechbolt, and magazine.

Purdey, James & Sons — Perhaps the most recognized name in double-barrel shotguns. Formed in 1814, Purdey makes only bespoke, made-to-order shotguns for an exclusive clientele. Purdey operates from the fashionable Mayfair district of London and has the reputation not only for making the world's finest shotguns but also for a haughty attitude that reflects its position among gunmakers.

Purdey underbolt — Developed in 1863 and more properly called a "sliding bolt," the Purdey underbolt is a sliding latch in the bottom of the action of a side-by-side or over/under that locks the barrels to the action by engaging the bites or notches in the barrel lumps. A very simple system, it is somewhat difficult to regulate, as there are two locking surfaces, one for the front bite and one for the rear bite, that should both make firm contact.

Pushbutton opener — Also called a lifter action, this is a style of locking mechanism common to older Parker shotguns. It operates by means of a small projection in front of the trigger guard that the shooter pushes up. The notch on the stem of the lifter, which holds the barrels closed, then rises enough to allow them to open. Upon closing, a spring snaps the lifter back down, clamping shut the breech. Although no longer seen on recently manufactured side-by-side shotguns, Lujtic shotguns, which are manufactured in the United States exclusively for trapshooting, use a pushbutton opener directly in front of the trigger guard.

Pushrod — A design attributed to John Deeley, the pushrod is one of several systems of securing the fore-end to the barrels using a long rod that extends through the fore-end and projects from its tip. Pushing the exposed end of the pushrod releases the fore-end latch. See **Anson & Deeley**.

Quail — A small upland bird, indigenous to North America, and, in the opinion of many, the most prized of upland game birds. Found wild, quail form coveys of from six to as many as fifteen birds. The classic quail is the bobwhite; other species include the scaled quail, Harlequin or Mearns' quail, and Gambel's quail.

Quail: *Quail are a favorite upland game bird in the United States, and many varieties are found from the Georgia pinewoods to the Arizona desert.*

Quail Unlimited — A conservation-oriented organization targeting habitat improvement and research to propagate quail throughout the United States.

Rabbit: *The "rabbit" is a tough clay target that is launched in such a way that it bounces sideways along the ground.*

Rabbit — **1.** The cottontail rabbit is one of the most popular upland game animals in the United States. **2.** A very hard, relatively thin clay target that bounces along the ground, simulating a bounding rabbit.

Rainbowing — In shooting, the habit of dropping the shoulder, causing the gun to rotate through an arc that resembles a rainbow. Rainbowing results in shooting behind the target. In right-handed shooters, rainbowing manifests itself in targets flying left to right; the opposite holds true for left-handed shooters. The cause of rainbowing is an overly wide stance as a result of which the shooter cannot swing from the feet up. Because only the upper body turns, the opposite shoulder (that is, the left in a right-handed shooter) pushes the gun shoulder down. The gun rotates from the horizontal, and although the shooter sees what looks like the correct lead, the shot goes behind the target.

Raising the head — Perhaps the most frequent fault in shotgun shooting. In the theory and practice of wingshooting, the shooter's eye is the rear sight of the shotgun. Any movement of the eye in relation to the comb and barrel rib results in an aiming error. There is an unconscious tendency among shooters to want to raise the head from its firm contact with the stock in order to see the target more clearly. This most often occurs with a premounted gun, as in American-style trap and skeet, but it can also occur in the field. Raising the head causes the shot to go high. The best cure is a well-fitted gunstock that provides the support necessary so that the shooter's head is most comfortable in place against the comb.

Range — **1.** The distance to a specific target, or the effective distance of a firearm. The shot from a 12-gauge shotgun firing target loads will drop within two hundred yards. Larger shot has a maximum range of about three hundred yards. However, the maximum *effective* range of any shotgun firing lead shot is about sixty-five yards, fifty yards for steel shot. There are those who advocate and claim kills at ranges in excess of sixty-five yards, but under careful scrutiny the ranges most frequently prove to be far shorter. The average shotgunner should attempt shots at no more than forty-five or fifty yards. **2.** A shooting facility or shooting range.

Rangoon Oil — A type of lubricating and rust-preventative oil popular in Great Britain through the 1970s. Although very traditional, it becomes gummy with long storage and often congeals into a hard mass over time. Replaced by synthetic lubricants, Rangoon Oil is now an anachronism.

Rational gunstock — A style of buttstock developed by W. W. Greener that never became popular. The Rational stock is essentially a Monte Carlo without the pronounced dip at the rear. In Greener's stock, the comb was straight to the point where the cheek made contact; it then dropped in a rounded manner to the butt. Not terribly attractive, this style of stock never won the favor of stock- and gunmakers.

The Rational Gun Stock.

Ready position — In the Churchill and other styles of shooting, a position in which the shooter brings the shotgun's butt into firm contact between the rib cage and upper arm, so that the gun is under full control for the mount itself.

Ready position: *This shotgunner, shooting sporting clays, shows a good ready position for a high crossing target. The butt is firmly under control between the rib cage and biceps, the muzzles in line with the eyes, and the body facing the direction in which target will appear. There is an overall appearance of relaxed tension in anticipation of the shot.*

Rebounding tumblers/hammers — A design for tumblers or hammers of a fixed-breech shotgun, either single- or double-barrel. Once they strike the primer (in the case of hammers with integral firing pins) or the firing pins, they rebound a fraction of an inch. Thus the firing pins will not remain embedded in the primer, which can make opening the shotgun difficult.

Recámera (Sp.) — "Chamber."

Receiver — Another term for the frame or action, most often related to the action of repeating shotguns—that is, pump-action and semiautomatic shotguns. See **action.**

Recoil — The rearward and upward movement of a firearm as a result of the discharge of the firearm and the ejection of the projectile, shot, wad, or other material from the muzzle. The effects of Newton's law of motion that states that for every action there is an equal and opposite reaction is evident in recoil. However, the shape of the buttstock, the weight of the firearm, the weight of the shot charge or projectile, muzzle brakes, style of action, and other factors will all modify recoil.

Greener's rule of ninety-six is perhaps the best guideline for gun weight. Simply put, a shotgun should be at least ninety-six times as heavy as the shot it fires. A shotgun shooting 1⅛ ounces of shot should weigh at least 6¾ pounds. A person shooting a one-ounce shot charge can comfortably shoot a shotgun weighing 6 pounds. However, when we approach the magnum charges, such as the currently fashionable two-ounce turkey load, a 12-pound gun is what you will need in order to have manageable recoil. Although gun weight is the prime factor in recoil, a properly shaped buttstock, especially one that directs the recoil downward, away from the cheekbones and directly into the heavy muscles of the shoulder, will do much to make recoil less intense. Semiautomatic actions spread out the perceived recoil, so that they, too, seem to recoil less than a fixed-breech gun of the same weight. Other devices such as muzzle brakes and barrel porting lessen recoil and partially or totally eliminate muzzle rise. The addition of weights to the fore-end, magazine tube, and buttstock will also lighten recoil. See **buttstock, porting, recoil reducer.**

Recoil-operated — A style of semiautomatic shotgun that depends upon the forces of recoil from the fired shell to operate the action. In this type of action, the barrel and breechbolt remain locked together as they both slide rearward under the force of the fired shell. When the breechbolt and barrel reach the rear of the receiver, the breechbolt is locked there while the barrel releases from the breechbolt and returns to its forward position, aided by a large spring that surrounds the magazine tube. As the barrel goes forward, the extractors on the breechbolt's face hold the fired shell and strip it from the chamber. A small ejector stud projecting from the rear of the barrel extension then kicks the fired shell free of the action through the ejection port. If there is a fresh round in the magazine, it releases as the barrel reaches its forwardmost position. The shell from the magazine moves rearward across the carrier and trips the carrier release, which, in turn, trips the bolt release. As the bolt moves forward, the carrier moves upward by means of a cam, raising the unfired shell to the level of the chamber, and the breechbolt pushes it home.

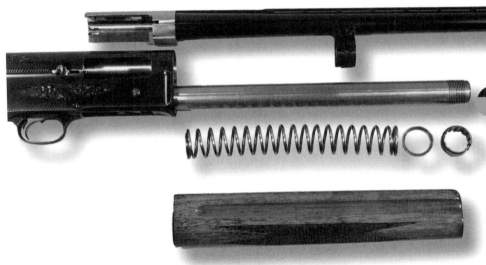

Recoil-operated: The parts of a Browning Automatic-5 recoil-operated semiautomatic shotgun. **(Top to bottom)** The barrel with the ring that surrounds the magazine tube and that compresses the friction ring, slowing the rearward movement of the barrel and bolt; the receiver and attached magazine tube, around which the barrel, friction rings, and barrel return spring move, and magazine cap; the barrel return spring, which also serves to slow recoil, and the two friction rings that surround the magazine tube and that apply friction to slow the barrel's rearward motion; the wooden fore-end.

The most copied and most successful of all recoil-operated shotguns was the Browning Automatic-5, the invention of John Moses Browning, first sold in 1905. Other recoil-operated shotguns were the Winchester Models 50 and 59, which used a slip chamber that recoiled only a fraction of an inch, setting in motion a heavy inertia block located in the buttstock. This inertia block pulled the bolt to the rear, ejecting the fired hull. If a fresh shell tripped the carrier release, it freed the bolt, the carrier moved upward, and the fresh shell entered the chamber. John Browning's son Val devised the Browning Double Automatic, which also worked on the short recoil principle. Other recoil-operated shotguns are the Sjörgren Normal, Remington II and II-48, and Franchi. See **automatic, Normal, semiautomatic.**

Recoil pad — A shotgun buttplate of rubber or synthetic material that absorbs some of the recoil. Most credit Walter Scott

Recoil Pad: *This American-style recoil pad by Pachmayr has a spacer and cavities. British recoil pads tend to be solid and often have no spacer.*

of Birmingham, England, with inventing the recoil pad, but it was Hugh Silver who refined the concept. Silver's pads monopolized the British gun trade during the late nineteenth century and well into the twentieth. Traditionally made of rubber, early pads such as the Silvers, Hawkins, and original Winchester pads are now available again as reproductions for those restoring a vintage shotgun. Perhaps the most familiar name is Pachmayr, who was among the first to mass-produce a full line of recoil pads. In recent years materials such as sorbothane, used as cushioning in jet aircraft ejection seats, have appeared in recoil pads, going by trade names such as Kick-Eez and the Pachmayr Decelerator®.

Recoil reducer, Edwards — A patented device using a spring-loaded mass within a tube. When installed in the buttstock of a shotgun, it attenuated recoil. Very popular among trapshooters, among whom Jesse Edwards was one, the device added weight. That in and of itself will lessen recoil—in some cases also drastically altering the balance of the gun.

Red-dot sight — An electronic sight that projects a red dot onto the optics. Placing the red dot upon a target (after zeroing, and variations notwithstanding) ensures that the shot will go where the red dot indicates. The Swedish AimPoint typifies this type of sight, which is useful for deer and turkey hunting.

Regulation of barrels — The art of boring and adjusting the barrels of a side-by-side or over/under so that they shoot to the same point of impact and print the prescribed pattern.

Reloading — 1. The practice of manufacturing one's own ammunition by replacing the main components of a spent shotshell: primer, propellant, wad, and shot. Various tools or machines are available to aid the reloader in making shotgun ammunition. See **handloading**. 2. The act of recharging the empty chambers and magazine of a firearm.

Remington — The oldest gunmaking company in the United States. Founded in 1816 by Eliphalet Remington II, the company still manufactures shotguns and rifles in Ilion, New York. Remington continues to manufacture two of the most popular repeating shotguns ever made, the 1100 gas-operated semiautomatic and the Model 870 pump action. Earlier classic shotguns by Remington include the Model 31 pump, which was the smoothest operating of any pump action ever manufactured; the Model 11 and 11-48, both recoil-operated semiautomatics; and the Model 32 and 3200 over/unders, which remain classic skeet and trap guns.

Remington currently manufactures shotshell and metallic cartridge ammunition at its plant in Lonoke, Arkansas. Originally Remington made only firearms, but in 1865 it bought two small ammunition companies, Crittenden & Tribbals and C. D. Leet & Company, which Remington merged into the Union Metallic Cartridge and Cap Company (later shortened to Union Metallic Cartridge Company, or U.M.C.) in Bridgeport, Connecticut. Remington subsequently acquired the Peters Victor Ammunition Company, operating it under the Peters name for a number of years. Currently, their ammunition carries the Remington name.

Remington lifter — Andrew E. Whitmore developed and patented the Remington lifter, which operated as a lever between the exposed hammers. Lifting it upward unlocked the breech. Remington used this type of action on side-by-side shotguns between 1874 and 1882, after which time the company moved to the more conventional top lever.

Report pair — In this combination of sporting clay targets, the trapper launches the first upon the shooter's call. The second target of the pair is released when the trapper hears the shooter fire at the first bird. See **sporting clays.**

Restriking — The act of refinishing the exterior of a set of barrels. Normally, polishing alone is not thought of as restriking. Barrels damaged by bulging, denting, or pitting, however, often need restriking before polishing.

Rib — A strip of metal running the length of a shotgun barrel as an aid to aligning the eye. Ribs can be attached to the barrel in various ways. Side-by-sides typically have solid ribs. Contemporary over/unders, pump actions, semiautomatics, and single-barrel trap guns will have ventilated ribs, which are ribs that sit on equally spaced posts, with open spaces between the bottom of the rib and the barrel. The idea behind ventilated ribs is that they will provide a smooth sighting plane and also diminish the occurrence of heat mirage during repeated firing or under hot conditions. Another term for solid ribs is matte ribs, a term especially prevalent for shotguns manufactured by Winchester Repeating Arms; matte ribs are found on Model 12 pumps and Model 21 doubles. Browning provided a very wide ventilated rib, the Broadway rib, to trapshooters on their Superposed over/unders. In British gunmaking, the swamped rib is a rib that is high at both the breech and muzzle ends of the barrels and low in-between.

Robert Churchill caused great controversy, some of which continues today, when he introduced his XXV, or 25-inch-barrel shotguns with the "Churchill rib." This rib tapers from breech to muzzle, and, in theory, gives the appearance of longer barrels when brought to the eye. Of course, if one is looking at the rib rather than the target, a miss is inevitable. Still and all, Churchill believed that his tapered rib compensated for the shortened sighting plane, although 25-inch barrels in themselves present a handling problem for all but the smallest shooter.

Ribs are also used to join side-by-side and over/under barrels. In the case of the side-by-side, the top rib serves the dual role of providing a sighting reference and holding the barrels together. There is also a rib on the bottom of a side-by-side, whose sole purpose is keeping the barrels solidly joined. Over/unders employ side ribs that hold the stacked barrels in alignment. Often these side ribs will be ventilated so as to allow cooling air to circulate. Some over/unders, such as the Remington 32, 3200, and Finnish-made Valmet, do not have side ribs, the barrels being held in place by the breech-end monobloc and a hanger at the muzzle. In theory, the barrels of these guns are free to expand and contract as they heat and cool. See **Monobloc.**

Rib extension — 1. An extension of the top barrel rib of a side-by-side shotgun that terminates in a doll's head, loop, or other shape, to provide either an additional or primary locking surface or added recoil absorption. **2.** An extension of a ventilated rib back over the receiver of a pump or semiautomatic shotgun. The most common example of this type of rib installation is the Winchester Model 12, in which the rib extended almost to the rear end of the receiver. Many of these Model 12 rib extensions terminate in what gunmakers refer to as a wide "duck's foot." See **doll's head, Greener crossbolt, Rigby-Bissel rising bite.**

Richards, Westley — See **Westley Richards under W.**

Rifling — The cutting of the inside surface of a gun barrel with grooves of a specific rate of twist from chamber mouth to muzzle. The grooves add stability to the trajectory of a projectile. In shotguns, which generally have smooth bores, rifled barrels are useful to hunters shooting sabot-style slugs at big game such as white-tailed deer. See **paradox gun, sabot slug.**

Rigby-Bissel rising bite — A type of third bite that uses a rib extension that is locked by a block that moves up and down within the standing breech. During unlocking, this block moves down so that the barrels will rotate; it then locks back into place as the barrels return to battery. See **battery, rib extension, third fastener.**

Ring bulge — The bulging of a shotgun barrel in a more-or-less even ring. Ring bulge occurs most often in shotguns with full-choked barrels in which the shooter fires steel shot. In that case, the bulge will be obvious to the naked eye, usually

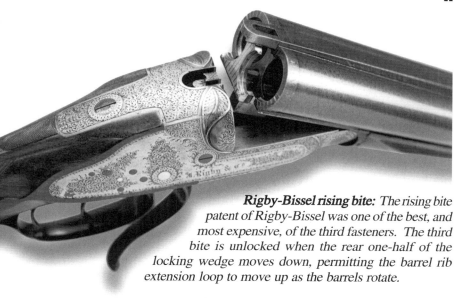

Rigby-Bissel rising bite: *The rising bite patent of Rigby-Bissel was one of the best, and most expensive, of the third fasteners. The third bite is unlocked when the rear one-half of the locking wedge moves down, permitting the barrel rib extension loop to move up as the barrels rotate.*

about a quarter- to a half-inch behind the muzzle. Steel shot typically causes a bulge of about 0.005 to 0.015 inch and then stops. However, in the case of a double-barrel shotgun, that is sufficient to cause barrel separation.

Ripon, Lord — (1852–1923) The Second Marquess of Ripon, also known as Earl de Grey, one of the greatest shots of the golden age of driven game shooting. If for no other reason, de Grey is memorable for shooting more game than anyone else, and keeping records of it. From 1867 to 1923, de Grey's game book records that he shot a total 124,193 partridge, 241,224 pheasant, and other game to a grand total of 556,813 heads of game over the course of 56 years. Reports have it that he killed 28 pheasants in one minute while shooting at the royal estate Sandringham, and on another occasion he reportedly had 7 dead birds in the air at the same time. Until his death in 1923, he used a garniture of three Purdey hammer guns. He died while out shooting after having made a double, a right and left, killing two grouse. There is little doubt that the motion picture *The Shooting Party* portrays de Grey correctly as being a fanatical shooter. It is reported that he practiced changing guns with his loaders late at night in order to improve the skills of his team. See *Shooting Party,* **Walsingham.**

Rolling — See **rainbowing.**

Roper, Sylvester — An American gunsmith, Roper received a patent on 10 April 1866, for a choking device. Applicable only to single-barrel guns, it was a ring that threaded onto the muzzle, providing some degree of constriction. Although this was very early in the development of choke, rings of varying degrees of

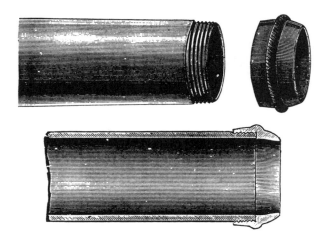

Roper's Detachable Choke-muzzle

constriction were presumably available. There is little evidence, however, of exactly what Roper offered. See **choke, Kimble, Pape.**

Rose and scroll — An elegant style of engraving that gunsmiths use on the finest side-by-sides.

Rotary underlever — A style of opener for a breechloading double gun that operates like a large screw. To open the breech, the shooter turns the lever, which is located on the bottom of the action, like a screw, and then swings down the barrels. To close the breech, the shooter swings up the barrels and screws the underlever back into the action, securing the barrels for firing. See **Jones underlever.**

Rottweil — Once imported into the United States by Dynamit Nobel-RWS, this shotgun was a popular international skeet gun for several years, but due to very limited distribution never became a mainstream shotgun in the United States. See **Dynamit Nobel RWS, Olympic skeet.**

Rough shooting — The British term for what Americans call upland hunting: walking the ground, usually with

Rough shooting: *Rather than standing and having the birds come to the guns, rough shooters walk the fields, often with pointing and flushing dogs.*

pointing or flushing dogs, in search of pheasant, partridge, quail, rabbit, or hare. It is an informal style of hunting, as opposed to the highly stylized driven hunt.

Round action — A style of boxlock action. John Dickson & Son in Edinburgh, Scotland, developed the Dickson round action, arguably one of the most elegant and graceful side-by-side shotguns ever made. Unique to this action is the fact that the ejector mechanism is in the body of the action, not in the fore-end as it is in virtually every other action. The firm remains in business to this day. See **action bar, Dickson, ejector, water table.**

Ruffed Grouse Society — One of several American conservation-oriented associations, the society is intent on furthering the understanding and habitat of the ruffed grouse.

SAAMI — See **Sporting Arms and Ammunition Manufacturers' Institute.**

Sabot (Fr.) — "Shoe." A type of shotgun round consisting of a solid projectile encased in a sabot or shoe that engages the bore or rifling, then peels away once the projectile has exited the muzzle. The purpose of a sabot is to center the projectile in the bore and engage the rifling. Used for hunting deer and animals of similar size, the sabot slug paired with a purpose-built rifled bore or rifled choke tube is nearly as accurate as a centerfire rifle. However, because of the relatively low muzzle velocity—1,300 to 1,550 feet per second—and the resulting high trajectory, even the best sabot slug/rifled shotgun combination has a maximum effective range of 100 to 125 yards.

Safety – 1. The catch that renders a firearm incapable of firing by means of the trigger. In most cases, the safety catch blocks only the trigger (or triggers) and does not prevent the hammers or tumblers from falling and discharging the shotgun if someone were to drop or severely jar it. However, most double shotguns of sidelock construction employ interceptor sears that have a second sear that will catch the hammer under those circumstances. Browning has used an interceptor sear in its semi-automatic 3½ Gold, and U.S. Repeating Arms/ Winchester has used a similar interceptor sear in its Super X 2, which it introduced in 1998. In any event, one should never rely upon a safety catch. Always be conscious of where your shotgun is pointing and never point it at anything you do not intend to shoot. See **interceptor/intercepting sear. 2.** Shotgun safety in general. The following points of safety apply regardless of the circumstance:

- Always treat every firearm as if it were loaded.
- Always verify that a firearm is unloaded when you first pick it up.
- Never point a firearm at anything you do not intend to shoot.
- Always pass a gun to another with the action or breech open and the barrels pointing in a safe direction.
- Always carry a shotgun with the action open until it is time to shoot.
- Never lay down a loaded shotgun or place one in a gun rack.
- Always make sure that you unload any unattended firearm and place it in such a way that nothing can knock it over.
- Never allow unsupervised youngsters to play with a firearm or ammunition and never leave firearms or shells where youngsters can find them.
- Never load a firearm indoors, except at a firing range.
- Always store firearms safely, in a secure cabinet or safe.
- Never place a loaded firearm in a vehicle.
- When in the field, always carry a firearm so that it does not and cannot point at a person or dog.
- Always unload a firearm when crossing a fence, stream, or other obstacle, even when you are alone.
- After crossing an obstacle, check that the barrels are free from obstructions before loading or reloading.
- Always keep fingers away from the triggers until you are ready to fire.
- Never rely on the safety catch.

Sauer, J. P., & Sohn — Currently affiliated with the Swiss firm SIG, Sauer has produced firearms in Eckernförde, Germany since 1751. Over the years, Sauer has manufactured European- or Continental-style side-by-sides, over/unders, and drillings.

Savage Arms, Inc. — A gunmaker primarily of rifles. In November 1929, Savage bought A. H. Fox and moved the Fox operation from Philadelphia to Utica, New York. Savage, who had acquired the J. Stevens firearm company in 1920, made a popular shotgun/rifle combination gun, and over the years they have produced utilitarian pump actions, semiautomatics, a copy of the Browning Auto-5, and side-by-sides. Savage manufactured the Fox Model B, and while it was a good, solid shotgun, it was not an A. H. Fox. For historical information regarding older Savage firearms, contact Mr. John Callahan, 53 Old Quarry Rd., Westfield, MA 01085, U.S.A. There is a nominal charge (fifteen dollars as of 1999) per gun for historical research by Callahan. See **Fox, A. H.**

Sawed-off shotgun — A shotgun whose barrels are shorter than the federally mandated minimum length. The possession of any shotgun with barrels shorter than 18 inches is regarded as a crime in the United States.

Sawn-off shotgun (Brit.) — See **sawed-off shotgun.**

Scalloping — The decorative cutting of scallops into the rear of a boxlock action where it meets the buttstock. Considered a sign of excellent craftsmanship, scalloping is usually evident only on high-quality boxlocks.

Schlagbolzen (Ger.) — "Firing pin."

Schnabel fore-end — A style of fore-end or forearm that terminates in a flared, decorative knob. Designed to allow the barrels to fit lower into the hand, the Schnabel fore-end originated in central Europe. Rifles and shotguns of European manufacture often use it, although recently manufacturers have begun to employ this style of fore-end on over/unders.

Scoring — 1. The gouging of a shotgun's bore by unprotected steel shot pellets. During the initial trials of steel shot, it became apparent that an extra-thick plastic shot cup was necessary in order to keep these extremely hard pellets from cutting into the bore. 2. Crude checkering in which the diamonds do not come to a point.

Scott, W. C. — One of the great Birmingham gunmakers. Since its founding in 1834, Scott produced excellent shotguns. Over the years, Scott, through mergers and amalgamations, variously used the names W. & C. Scott, W. C. Scott & Sons, and Webley & Scott.

Holland & Holland ultimately purchased the firm in 1985, with the idea that Scott would produce essentially machine-made shotguns under the Holland & Holland name. Ultimately, production substantially slowed, and in 1991 Scott's operations ceased altogether.

Scott spindle — Created and patented by Birmingham's W. C. Scott & Sons, this is the standard top lever common to all current side-by-side and over/under shotguns. This locking system combined the Purdey underbolt, the Scott spindle, and the familiar top lever unto a unified whole that has remained a success for decades. See **top lever.**

Screwdriver — Anyone contemplating the removal or tightening of the screws on a firearm must acquire a screwdriver (Brit., turnscrew) that exactly fits each screw's slot, both in terms of depth and width. An ill-fitting screwdriver can irreparably burr the screw heads, a type of damage that significantly reduces the value of the gun. See **turnscrew.**

Screw-in chokes — Although Winchester pioneered the modern screw-in choke (Roper made screw-on choke rings in 1866),

it was not until the late 1970s that screw-in chokes became part of shotgun shooting. Many regard this as the most significant improvement in shotguns since the perfection of the double gun in the 1800s and the introduction of pump-action in the late 1890s, and

Screw-in chokes: An example of a full set of screw-in chokes, in this instance by Briley Manufacturing, Houston, Texas. Included is a Briley speed wrench that enables the shooter to change chokes in a few seconds.

semiautomatic shotguns in the early years of the twentieth century.

Screw-in chokes are installed by reaming and threading the interior of the muzzle to accept a particular brand or style of choke tube (i.e., Briley, Browning/Winchester Invector-Plus, etcetera), and then the shooter can regulate his patterns to virtually any shooting situation by simply removing one tube and substituting another. Many aftermarket companies such as Briley Manufacturing, Seminole, and Stan Baker offer custom screw-in choke installation and also tubes that are compatible with factory-threaded barrels. See **choke, Roper.**

Sear — The all-important part of any firearm that connects the trigger with the tumbler or hammer. When the shooter pulls the trigger, a mechanical linkage lifts or drops the sear from its engagement with the sear notch, allowing the spring to drive the hammer or tumbler forward to hit the striker or firing pin and discharge the gun. See **bent, hammer/tumbler, interceptor/intercepting sear, sear notch, trigger.**

Sear notch — The notch in the hammer that the nose of the sear engages upon cocking. It is this engagement that prevents the shotgun from firing until the shooter pulls the trigger.

Tumbler or Hammer

Sear

Sear Notch

With finely tuned sears, trigger pull is crisp and light. Currently, manufacturers design shotguns with a very heavy sear engagement to prevent accidental discharge by dropping or jarring. Only a competent gunsmith should make adjustments to the trigger pull. If shotgunners were aware of the very small amount of contact the sear has, they would be less likely to rely on the safety catch. With some exceptions (sidelocks with interrupting sears and, at this time, the Browning Gold series and Winchester Super X 2 semiautomatics, which employ an interrupting sear) the safety does nothing more than block the trigger from contacting the sear lifter. See **bent, intercepting sear, sear.**

Season — The time of the year when hunters may take specific game animals.

Second or intercepting sear — See **interceptor/intercepting sear.**

Secretario (Sp.) — The individual that serves as supervisor of the various pickup persons and loader at a driven shoot in Spain.

Security/safety lock — A means of rendering a firearm incapable of firing without first disengaging the lock. These take two forms. One employs a keyed or electronically operated device that covers the trigger guard, making it impossible to access the trigger. The other is a locking cable that runs through the ejection port of a repeating shotgun to prevent closing of the action upon a live round.

Selective ejector — See **ejector.**

Self-opening — A style of double-barrel shotgun that uses the main spring or carries a strongly sprung plunger device in the fore-end to self-open. When the top lever rotates, the main spring acting through a cam or the plunger pushes the barrels down into the open position, simultaneously ejecting the fired cartridges and cocking the tumblers or hammers. While this style of double shotgun sounds appealing, it is worth noting that these shotguns are hard to close, since the heavy spring is not easy to compress.

Semiautomatic — See **autoloader.**

Semiautomatique (Fr.) — "Semiautomatic."

Semiautomatico (Ital.) — "Semiautomatic."

Semiautomatic: *Four gas-operated semiautomatic shotguns.* **(Left to right)** *Mossberg 9200, Beretta A 390, Remington Euro-Lightweight, Browning Gold.*

Serial number — The unique identifying number that manufacturers stamp into the metal of the action or receiver of a firearm. Many shotguns, especially double shotguns, will also have the serial number stamped on the barrels, fore-end, and buttstock. A portion of the serial number will also be on the locks and other smaller subassemblies. Many shotguns, however, have no serial numbers; an example is the Winchester Model 37 single-barrel shotgun. Many nineteenth-century Damascus-barrel double guns also have no numbers. In some instances, serial numbers can be useful in tracing dates of manufacture, but loss of factory records often leaves serial number dating to conjecture.

Service pressure — A set of pressure parameters from the Sporting Arms and Ammunition Manufacturers' Institute (SAAMI) that closely correspond to the standards of the International Proof Commission (C.I.P.). The goal is to ensure that ammunition for

Gauge	Chamber length in inches	Maximum service pressure in pounds per square inch
10	3 ½	11,000 psi
12	3 ½	14,000 psi
12	3	11,500 psi
12	2 ¾	11,500 psi
16	2 ¾	11,500 psi
20	3	12,000 psi
20	2 ¾	12,000 psi
28	2 ¾	12,500 psi
.410	3	13,500 psi
.410	2 ½	12,500 psi

various firearms does not exceed a safe level of pressure in common use. The following are the service pressures SAAMI has established by means of modern piezoelectric transducers. Because of the different technique involved, these data do not compare directly to data resulting from tests with copper and lead crushers.

Shot — Projectiles designed for use in shotguns. Originally, all shot was of lead in various sizes, from large buckshot to extremely fine number 12 shot for use in .22-caliber rifles to control small pests. To lead, manufacturers add varying amounts of antimony— 0.5 to 7 percent—which hardens the lead and, more important, serves as a surface-tensioning agent so that the pellets form round spheres as they drop in the shot tower. Use of nontoxic shot has recently become law in many parts of the world for waterfowl hunting; some countries, such as Denmark, require it for all shotgun hunting. Originally, steel shot was the only approved nontoxic shot. More recently bismuth, tungsten/polymer, and tin shot have appeared as approved alternatives to steel. See **nontoxic shot, pellet size, shot tower.**

Shot: *On left are ultra-round hard steel pellets; on right are dropped lead pellets.*

Shot sizes — Although shot sizes differ very little throughout the world, there are some variations between traditional American and British shot sizes. The table shows the slight variations. Note that as manufacturers tighten their offering, some of these shot sizes may no longer be commercially available.

Shot size in inches	American	British
0.338		LG
0.360	000	
0.347		MG
0.330	00	
0.332		SG
0.320	0	
0.300	No. 1	
1.298		Special SG
0.270	No. 2	
0.269		SSG
0.250	No. 3	
0.245		SSSG
0.240	No. 4	
0.227		SSSSG
0.220	F (steel)	
0.214		SSSSSG
0.203		AAA
0.200	T (steel)	
0.194		AA
0.190	BBB (steel)	
0.180	BB	A
0.177	air rifle	
0.170		BBB
0.161		BB
0.160	1 (steel)	
0.154		B
0.150	2	
0.143		1
0.140	3 (steel)	

Shot size in inches	American	British
0.140	3 (steel)	
0.135		2
0.130	4	
0.128		3
0.120	5	4
0.110	6	5
0.107		5½
0.102		6
0.099		6½
0.095	7½	7
0.090	8	
0.087		8
0.085	8½	
0.080	9	9
0.070		10
0.050	12	

Shot string — When a shooter fires a shotshell, the shot exits the muzzle as an elongated, sausage-shaped cluster. In general, the tighter the choke, the shorter this sausage-shaped string; the more open the choke, the longer this string. Results at the patterning board suggest a flat, pancakelike cluster of shot, but all shot strings to one degree or another. Bob Brister, in his book *Shotgunning: The Art and Science*, explored shot stringing using paper targets mounted on a frame attached to a boat trailer that was towed at various speeds. He reported that steel shot, because it does not deform and hence flies true to the target, seems to string very little.

If everyone were a highly accomplished shot, stringing might not be important. However, because of a shotgun's application to shooting moving targets, shot stringing adds an extra dimension to the effectiveness of the shot. Because of this three-dimensional pattern, which has both an effective width at a given yardage as well as a depth into which the bird or clay target can fly, the marksman has the luxury of being able to lead a bit too much and still hit the quarry as it flies into the column of shot. This, of course, in no way compensates for a shot fired behind the target. In the days before plastic shot-protecting wads, shot stringing was a big advertising issue amongst the various ammunition companies. While it is still an issue, because of the protection afforded lead shot by shot cups and buffering and because of the use of steel shot, shot strings are far shorter now than they were in the days of soft shot, card, and felt wads.

Shotgun — A smoothbore firearm designed to shoot multiple projectiles. Shotguns come in various styles: single-barrel, side-by-side, over/under double-barrel, bolt-action, semiautomatic, pump-action, and combination shotgun/rifles. Specialized shotguns with partially or fully rifled barrels are made for shooting single projectiles at big game. Other big-game applications include the use of a shotgun with buckshot for pursuing wounded thin-skinned game such as leopard and lion. Apart from these unique big-game applications—and the more common use of smoothbore shotguns for shooting single projectiles called rifled slugs—the shotgun is primarily a gun for shooting moving targets with charges of shot. See **action, buckshot, pellet size.**

Shooting school — A school that offers shooting instruction and gun fitting. Whether it is at a permanent location or wherever a traveling instructor sets up shop, the value of shooting instruction cannot be overestimated. Although the practice was originally British, various Americans have set themselves up as shooting instructors. Unfortunately, only a few are at the level of their British counterparts. However, any instruction is normally beneficial, as an instructor can often spot flaws in the shooter's technique and help correct the problem. Gunfitting is another benefit of the shooting school. A highly experienced instructor can efficiently fit a particular shooter, and suggest corrections to an existing shotgun that will make mounting the shotgun easier and greatly improve marksmanship.

Shooting school: *Ken Davies, Holland & Holland's chief instructor, coaches a student at a shooting grounds near Columbia, South Carolina.*

Shooting Party, The — A novel by the British author Isabel Colgate that explores the social mores and shooting etiquette of British society on the eve of World War I. The book later became a motion picture starring the late James Mason (it was his last film appearance) and Sir John Gielgud. The film features some very bad shooting form yet portrays much of the society, etiquette, and shooting decorum of the day.

Shot tower — A building approximately 150 feet tall in which the machinery to make lead shot is located. At the very top is a furnace and a set of sieves, each precisely perforated for each different size of shot made. With the appropriate sieve in place, lead and a small amount of antimony—from 3 to 6 percent, depending on the harshness of shot to be dropped—is melted in the furnace, then poured through the sieve. The globules of lead/antimony alloy fall through the air, and because of the surface-tensioning effect of the antimony, spheres are formed, which ultimately drop into a pool of water at the bottom of the tower. From there, the shot is raised by elevator partway back up the tower, where it is poured across a series of inclined plates constructed with gaps between them. If the shot is perfectly round, it will roll with sufficient velocity to jump over the gaps. However, out-of-round shot and pellets fused into clumps will not roll fast enough to bridge these gaps and will fall into a recovery bin. The round shot is then either sent to the loading machines, in the case of an ammunition company, or to be bagged for distribution and sale to handloaders.

Shoulder pocket — The area in which to place the shotgun's butt each time you mount a shotgun. Find it by raising your arm until the bottom of the forearm and upper arm are parallel with the ground and your hand is in front of you. With the arm in that position, feel for the small depression between the collarbone and shoulder. It is in this slight depression that the butt should rest in a proper gun mount.

Side-by-side — A twin or double shotgun whose barrels lie horizontally. This is the classic game gun, but in the past several decades the over/under has superseded it in popularity. The side-by-side offers a wide sighting plane, instant choice between two chokes, and, in all but the lowest grade of shotgun, excellent between-the-hands balance.

Side-by-side: (Left to right) *Exposed-hammer 10-bore waterfowl gun; boxlock game gun; sidelock game gun.*

Side-by-side: *The evolution of the side-by-side shotgun.* **(Top to bottom)** *Muzzleloading percussion; breechloading exposed hammer; hammerless sidelock; and boxlock.*

Side clips — In a side-by-side shotgun, small protruding extensions on the sides of the action balls, fence, or standing breech that mate with a matching cut on the sides of the breech end of the barrels. The function of these side clips is to provide extra strength and to eliminate side-to-side movement of the barrels during firing. In practice, however, they are superfluous unless the maker has fitted them very carefully. Even bespoke guns of recent manufacture rarely employ them.

Side lever — One of several possible placements for the opening lever on a breechloading side-by-side shotgun. The lever normally lies along the right side of the action, and pushing it down opens the breech. Some guns have the lever on the left side, as some shooters prefer.

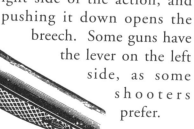

Sidelock — Employing a design that gunmakers originally carried over from flint- and percussion-lock shotguns, the sidelock shotgun carries all of the firing mechanism on plates that the manufacturer inlets into the head of the stock and action bar. All that is within the head of the buttstock and action is the safety catch lever, the strikers or firing pins, the top lever that opens the action, and the trigger or triggers. All else—mainspring, sear, intercepting sear, and tumbler, or hammer—is carried on the side plate.

There are two variations of the sidelock: back action and bar action. In the first, the mainspring lies behind the hammer, with the lockwork basically within the wood of the buttstock. The bar action places the mainspring ahead of the trigger, within the action bar. All currently manufactured side-by-side sidelock shotguns are bar action, in the style of the Purdey or Holland & Holland sidelock.

Sidelock: *Comparing the sidelock* **(above)** *and the boxlock* **(below)**.

In general, quality sidelocks offer better trigger pulls than a boxlock, and they have the added advantage of interceptor sears, a decided safety benefit. Sidelocks are also easy to remove to clean and lubricate. However, in terms of function, the sidelock is little superior to a good boxlock. In addition, boxlocks tend to be more robust and seldom fail, whereas sidelocks will more often break the leaf mainsprings at the most inopportune time; while repairing them is easy, the job can cost more than a few minutes during a drive or hunt. See **action, back action, bar action, boxlock, interceptor/interrupting** sears.

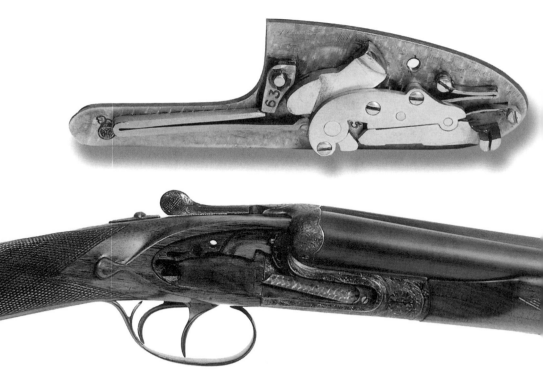

Sidelock: *The internal works of a Holland & Holland-style sidelock. The hammer or tumbler spring, hammer, and sears are visible. Gold plate on the moving parts prevents rust.*

Side plate — A nonfunctional plate on the rear side of a boxlock action that gives the impression the gun is a sidelock. Under honorable circumstances, these side plates offer a broad canvas for engraving. Under less than honorable circumstances, they can fraudulently serve to represent a shotgun as a true sidelock when, in fact, it isn't. The key is to look for the pins around which the tumblers or hammers revolve and that serve as screws for affixing the various parts of the lock to the side plate. If such pins are absent, the gun is a boxlock made to resemble a sidelock—but not functionally so. See **false side plate.**

Sighting plane — The area from the shooter's eye to the end of the muzzle or muzzles. Adding a flat rib that extends from the breech to the muzzle brings this plane into better focus. Remember, however, that concentrating on the rib, barrel, or front sighting bead will nearly always result in a miss. See **bead, rib.**

Sights — Devices affixed to the receiver, action, or barrel of a shotgun as an aid to marksmanship. During World War II, gunners assigned to bombers trained with a shotgun sight that gave them a feel for the radial in use on aircraft machine guns. Called the Nydar sight, these were available as surplus items following the war. Recently, sights projecting a red dot or holographic image have become popular with pistol competitors; and there are also some applications for shotgunners, especially deer hunters who shoot slugs and turkey hunters who try to place a very tight charge of shot into the head of a strutting turkey. Other types of sights include beads of various colors, luminescent or fluorescent beads that glow in the dark, and ribs. See **bead, mid bead, Nydar sight, rib.**

Simmons, Ernie, Sr. (1903–1970) — The Olatha, Kansas, gunsmith who pioneered aftermarket ventilated ribs and other gunsmithing services. At one time, Simmons subcontracted the installation of ventilated ribs on Model 12 and Model 42 shotguns for Winchester.

Simultaneous pair — In sporting clays shooting, two targets launched at the same instant. They may be crossing targets or they may fly in the same direction. Also called a true pair. See **sporting clays.**

Single trigger — A shotgun trigger that fires both barrels, one after the other, of a double-barrel shotgun. Early single triggers were plagued with problems, mostly the tendency to double—that is, to fire both barrels at the same time. Makers have overcome that problem, and seldom does a modern single-trigger double; if it does, it is a signal to have the gun inspected by a competent gunsmith. With the exception of the least expensive shotguns, or some bespoke shotguns whose owners specify a nonselective trigger, all shotguns today come with a single trigger and some kind of barrel-selection device. Some of these are awkward, others less so, but the major failing of single triggers is the need to manipulate a button or lever to change the firing order. See **barrel selector, trigger.**

16-gauge — A shotgun with a bore measuring 0.662 inch and through which sixteen one-ounce lead balls can pass. The 16-gauge was at one time very popular with American upland bird hunters and European hunters, and it was often the gauge of choice for the shotgun barrel(s) of a combination gun. In recent decades the 16-gauge has continued to lose popularity through the promotion of the 20-gauge as a lighter shotgun that is capable of shooting the same shot charge of 1 or 1 1/8 ounces of shot. However, older 16-gauge shotguns constructed by Parker, A. H. Fox, or some British and European manufacturers on a proper 16-gauge frame with appropriately light barrels are wonderful upland bird and dove guns; knowledgeable hunters still seek them out. Unfortunately, ammunition sales have now sagged to the point that the major ammunition manufacturing companies catalog a bare minimum of loads for this wonderful gauge. See **combination gun, gauge.**

SKB — A line of shotguns from SKB Arms Company, Tokyo, Japan, an arms producer since 1855. SKB shotguns are sturdy, well-built guns that incorporate reinforced actions reminiscent of the German Merkel.

Skeet — An archaic Scandinavian word meaning "to shoot." Co-devised by Charles E. Davies of Andover, Massachusetts, skeet began as an informal game that involved one trap; the shooters moved around a circle. Davis named his game "Shooting around the Clock." A neighbor's complaints later caused him to cut the circle in half and add a second trap opposite the original one, which he eventually raised to add variety. Soon publicity began to promote this new, more casual game that better simulated shooting upland birds in the field than did more formal trapshooting.

In 1920, Davies's friend William Harnden Foster, who had been an original participant in Shooting around the Clock, became editor of *National Sportsman*, perhaps the most popular such magazine of its day. Foster promoted the game, and by 1926 Davies had set down the rules; yet the game lacked a good name. Foster sponsored a contest in *National Sportsman* and its sister publication *Hunting and Fishing*, offering a prize of one hundred dollars for the best name. Gertrude Hurlbutt of Dayton, Montana, won the prize with her submission of "skeet." Today skeet has become as formal and rigid as trapshooting, but it remains a good way to keep your shooting skills sharp. The competition draws many who do not hunt.

American-style skeet takes place on a field with eight shooting positions arranged around a half-circle; the eighth position is midway between the two traps. Targets fly from the "high house" and "low house." At each station, shooters shoot one target from the high house and one from the low. On stations one (directly under the high-house trap), two, six, and seven (which is just to

Skeet shooting

the side of the low-house trap), shooters fire at targets released simultaneously. The traps launch targets at an angle such that the targets cross six yards outside of station eight, which offers a quick, incoming target. When the shooters call "pull," the target must appear within one second; most "grooved" shooters demand an almost instantaneous target. Since 1954, premounting the gun has been permissible, all leading to the quest for perfection. A visible piece must separate from a target in order for it to count as a hit or dead target. Any target from which the referee does not see a visible piece fly counts as lost.

There are five separate events in skeet: 12-gauge, 20-gauge, 28-gauge, .410-bore, and doubles. In recent years, skeet has become a game of perfection, with one hundred-straights run in almost every competition. To break ties, it became necessary to begin shooting doubles—two targets released at the same moment at each station. Even then, many top shooters will shoot 100 or 200 doubles before a winner emerges. Competitions normally are for 100 targets, sometimes in only one or two gauges at small club competitions. At large regional, state, and national competitions, the 12-gauge competition normally involves 250 targets.

Olympic-style skeet employs a much faster target, which a computer releases at intervals varying from instantaneously (as in current American-style skeet) up to a delay of as much as three seconds (as it was in the original version of skeet). In addition, shooters do not shoot doubles at stations one and seven, but rather at positions two, three, five, and six. The butt of the shotgun must remain visible below the dropped elbow until the target emerges, making excellent, consistent gun-mounting a primary requirement. The governing body of skeet in the United States is the National Skeet Shooting Association.

Skeleton buttplate — A carefully crafted, blued, or case-hardened steel rim that encloses the butt of a shotgun, preventing the splitting or breaking of the butt, most especially the toe.

Sleeved barrels — The process of cutting off the existing barrels of a shotgun in front of the chamber, then boring out the chamber area—essentially forming a monobloc—to accept a new set of barrels. The gunsmith then brazes or silver-solders the barrels into the newly formed monobloc, reattaches the top and bottom ribs, and regulates the barrels as to point of impact and pattern percentage. After bluing, the gun is ready to go. By this sleeving method, many unshootable or severely damaged shotguns take on a new life. See **bluing, monobloc, regulation of barrels.**

Sleeved chamber — The chamber of a shotgun into which a gunsmith has inserted a permanent steel sleeve so that the gun can be used with the next-smaller size cartridge. In this process, it is necessary to sleeve the chamber to a smaller gauge—that is, a 10-bore becomes a 12 and a 12-gauge becomes a 20-gauge. Sleeves are appropriate only for barrels that are in good condition and relatively free of deep pitting.

Sling — A strap that allows one to carry a shotgun over the shoulder. Their use was formerly a European tradition, and one seldom saw a shotgun with a sling, or provisions for using a sling, in the United States. However, waterfowl, deer, and turkey hunters have more recently embraced slings as a means of carrying their shotgun, leaving the hands free for decoys and so forth. Currently, repeating shotguns specifically for waterfowl, deer, and turkey hunting come equipped with sling swivels; some have slings attached.

Slug — A single, solid projectile of soft lead that hunters use primarily for white-tailed deer, but that can be equally effective on other soft-skinned big game of small to medium size. Slugs originated as round "pumpkin balls," later becoming the Foster-style slug, a hollow-based, conical projectile with angled striations on the side. Upon firing, the base of the Foster-style slug expands to a tight fit in the shotgun's bore; the striations supposedly catch the bore, causing the slug to spin like a projectile from a rifled bore. Variations such as the Brenneke slug, a German-made slug with wads attached to its base, provide better velocity and accuracy. Most recently, sabot-encased slugs have become the projectile of choice for hunters. Encased in a plastic sabot, or shoe, these slugs are for use in partially or fully rifled barrels and provide excellent accuracy. Due to their very high trajectory, rifled slugs of any variety have a limited effective range of 75 to 125 yards. The best combination is a scope-sighted, rifled-barrel shotgun zeroed at 100 yards. With such a gun the hunter can hold dead on out to 100 yards. Beyond that range, the drop is too rapid for the slug to be of much use. See **paradox gun, rifling, sabot.**

Slug gun — A shotgun specifically for shooting slugs at big game such as white-tailed deer. Currently, these shotguns come with fully rifled barrels intended for use with sabot slugs and holes drilled and tapped for the installation of a scope or other style sight. See **rifling, sabot.**

Slug gun: *The Savage 210F bolt-action, a shotgun for shooting sabot slugs at white-tailed deer. This style of shotgun has a fully rifled barrel.*

Small-gauge conversion tubes — Gauge-specific tubes of aircraft-grade aluminum, with steel or titanium chambers, that fit into a side-by-side or over/under shotgun, making it capable of firing cartridges of a smaller gauge. Skeet shooters frequently make use of conversion tubes; a shooter using a 12-gauge shotgun equipped with small-gauge tubes in 20- and 28-gauge and .410-bore can use the same gun for all four events. Hunters, likewise, can adapt a 12- or 20-gauge shotgun to a smaller gauge. The use of these tubes comes with one drawback, however: weight. Even a light set of tubes adds a pound or more. Currently, Briley Manufacturing in Houston, Texas, is the world's largest producer of full-length conversion tubes.

Smith, Jeremiah — Perhaps the true inventor of choke boring. J. W. Long, in his *American Wildfowling,* states, "I have the most positive and reliable proof of its [choke boring's] having been practiced in this country [the United States], according to the most approved manner of the present day, over fifty years ago; the earliest person to whom I have been able to trace a knowledge of it being Jeremiah Smith, a gunsmith, of Southfield, R.I., who discovered its merits in 1827." See **choke, Kimble, Pape, Roper.**

Snap caps — Dummy cartridges useful for practice and for storage of shotguns. With a snap cap in the chamber, you can drop the hammer without risking damage to the firing pin. Metal or plastic snap caps resemble a shotshell of the same gauge. However, in place of the primer there is a piece of hard plastic or rubber that absorbs the impact of the striker. Available at gun shops, snap caps may cost as little as a few dollars for a pair of plastic caps or may be quite expensive, for an engraved metal pair by a well-known gunmaker. For the double-gun enthusiast, a pair of snap caps for each gun is a necessity.

Snap caps.

Snap caps in 12- and 28-gauge.

Snap action — A double-barrel shotgun action that shuts with a snap. All contemporary actions are snap actions: When the shooter closes the barrels the locking bolt and opening lever—the top lever—snap into the locked position.

Snap underlever — An early method of opening the action of a double-barrel shotgun with a lever located below the trigger guard that operated with a snap-style closing.

Snaphaunce — The immediate predecessor of the flintlock. The name derives from the Danish *snaphaan*, literally "snapping hen" or "pecking rooster," describing the action of the hammer.

Soft shot — A colloquialism used to describe dropped shot that has a very low antimony content. Popular with quail hunters, soft shot, especially before the universal use of plastic shot protectors, deformed easily and therefore provided very wide, close-range patterns. See **dropped shot, lead shot.**

Solid frame — A repeating shotgun that does not come apart for cleaning or transportation. Examples of solid-frame guns are the early pump-action Winchester Model 1897 and the later Model 25. The disadvantages of this type of gun are minor, although a solid-frame repeater is much harder to clean than a take-down model. The gun is no sturdier than any other.

Solid rib — A rib on a shotgun barrel that does not have posts or spacers for ventilation. Most commonly seen on side-by-sides and many Winchester Model 12 repeaters. Matte rib is another term for solid rib. See **rib**.

Sorbothane — A modern, impact-absorbing material that protects military fighter pilots from the severe impact of ejecting from an aircraft. Also common in recoil pads, sorbothane is an excellent choice for anyone sensitive to recoil, or who shoots primarily heavy field and magnum loads.

Sousa, John Philip (1854–1932) — Perhaps America's most famous composer and bandmaster. During his lifetime, he publicly embraced hunting and trapshooting. Sousa developed much positive publicity for the shooting sports whenever he attended a trapshoot. In addition, he vigorously promoted hunting. At one time, Sousa, along with the DuPont family, owned a large tract of land in South Carolina that they reserved specifically for hunting. For many years Sousa shot at the Grand American trapshoot, and he continued to shoot with one arm after injuring his neck in a fall from his horse Patrician Charlie. He traditionally fired the first shot at the Grand American, and Ithaca produced a highly engraved, top-of-the-line single-barrel trap gun in his honor called the Sousa Grade, of which only eleven were made.

Sousa-garde (Fr.) — "Fore-end."

Southgate ejectors — A type of ejector mechanism very similar to the one used in most modern side-by-sides.

Speed of flight — The following are average flight speeds for various game birds:

Bird	Flight speed in feet per second	Average speed in feet per second
Bobwhite quail	60 to 80	70
Ruffed grouse	65 to 80	72.5
Mourning dove	70 to 90	80
Mallard duck	50 to 90	70
Canvasback duck	90 to 100	95
Canada goose	80 to 90	85

Sperm oil — Oil from the blubber of sperm whales. At one time many considered it the finest oil for lubricating locks. With environmentalist opposition to whaling and the development of various superior synthetic lubricants, sperm oil is now but a memory.

Spindle — The link between the top lever and locking or bolting system of a double gun.

Sporting Arms and Ammunition Manufacturers' Institute — Best known by its abbreviation SAAMI, this organization, whose funds come from sporting arms and ammunition manufacturers, establishes standards for all items pertaining to sporting firearms and ammunition in the United States. These standards include chamber and bore dimensions, acceptable service pressures, proof-load pressures, and so forth. SAAMI assumes much of the function of the various foreign proof houses regarding the common establishment of standards. However, SAAMI does not test firearms, leaving that to the individual manufacturers. See **pressure, service pressure.**

Sporting clays — A clay target game that closely simulates the hunting of wild birds and game animals. Courses are laid out using as much of the existing terrain as possible, with the idea of duplicating what live game would do if flushed there. As with skeet, sporting clays has established a following that views it more as a competitive game than as a means of improving marksmanship. Targets include bounding rabbits, springing teal, foxes, pheasants, quail, grouse, and double releases that simulate two birds or a bird and rabbit, in the form of simultaneous, following, and report pairs. The selection of targets is somewhat dependent upon the terrain and features of the course.

Commonly, the shotgun of choice for sporting clays is the 12-gauge over/under with interchangeable, screw-in chokes. Those sensitive to recoil frequently choose the 20-gauge, and few are the targets that cannot be broken with the smaller-gauge gun. At many large competitions,

Sporting clays: *This shooting sport challenges the shooter with clay targets of various sizes, representing game animals in the field. A competitive sport in its own right, sporting clays is a fun way to maintain and improve shooting skills.*

there are added events for side-by-sides, hammer guns, and small gauges—the 28-gauge and .410-bore—to add interest. Another variation of sporting clays is five-stand, in which shooters fire from five positions at various targets familiar from regular courses. Frequently, skeet fields can become five-stand setups with the addition of extra, strategically placed traps.

The following are the current governing bodies for sporting clays competition. *English sporting clays:* Clay Pigeon Shooting Association, Earlstrees Court, Corby, Northants, UK NN17 4AX. *American sporting clays,* which for bizarre reasons has two associations: National Sporting Clays Association, 5931 Roft Road, San Antonio, Texas 78253; Sporting Clays of America, 9257 Buckeye Road, Sugar Grove, Ohio 43155-9632. See **following pair, report pair, simultaneous pair.**

Spreader load — A shotshell, usually exclusively in 12-gauge, intended to throw a very wide pattern when shot from a full-choked shotgun. In the first two-thirds of the twentieth century, most shotguns manufactured and sold in the United States were full-choked. Hunters who wished to use their full-choked shotgun for quail, woodcock, ruffed grouse, or other close-flushing game could use a spreader or brush load in order to have a more open pattern for this close-range shooting. Brush or spreader loads were constructed using compartmented wads, either horizontal or vertical, to separate the shot, and in later developments a post located in the center of plastic shot cups.

Spreader wad — A wad or wad insert whose function is to throw open patterns from a tightly choked shotgun. These wads are often of one-piece plastic construction with a solid post projecting from the bottom of the shot cup. Other variations are thin cardboard cruciform inserts that divide the shot column in the shot cup into four equal sections; some wads divide the shot charge horizontally. See **brush load, spreader load.**

Springs — The basic component of any firearm that propels the hammer or tumbler, causing the gun to fire. Springs are of two basic styles: coil, and leaf or V. Coil springs are far more reliable, insofar as they tend not to break, and often will continue to function even if broken. They do weaken with time and deliver diminishing energy as they weaken. Leaf or V springs are more traditional, more powerful, and a bit faster, but they are more prone to breakage.

Stanbury, Percy — For many years the late Percy Stanbury was the chief instructor at the West London Shooting Grounds. He taught a slightly different approach to shooting than did the late Robert Churchill. In the Churchill style, the shooter's weight shifts from foot to foot, while Stanbury felt that the feet should remain still, with the weight primarily over the front foot and the rear heel slightly lifted. Stanbury taught that most of the swing should be from the waist, while Churchill taught swing from the feet. In reality, Stanbury was tall and slim, Churchill short and stocky, and each style fit its progenitor. Both styles are equally good and each has its followers. During his lifetime, Stanbury won almost every shooting title in Great Britain, all with a 30-inch-barrel Webley & Scott side-by-side choked full in both barrels.

Stance — The all-important starting point for good shooting. Most instructors will teach shooters to assume a stance with the feet about shoulder width apart and the weight evenly balanced between the feet. See **foot position.**

Standing breech — The vertical portion of the action of a double- or single-barrel shotgun. It is against the standing breech that the heads of the cartridges rest when in the chamber. The firing pin(s) or striker(s) protrude through holes in the standing breech. See **breakoff, detonating.**

Steel shot — The first successful nontoxic pellet approved for taking waterfowl in the United States, Canada, and Europe. Although considerably lighter than lead, these pellets can provide consistent kills within about 40 yards.

Because steel shot is about 30 percent lighter than lead, the next-larger pellet size must be chosen to provide the same approximate lethality. Hence, if a duck hunter shot No. 4 lead, he would then choose No. 2 steel. Goose hunters found that it was necessary to use very large steel-shot pellets in the range of BB, BBB, and T in order to ensure positive kills on Canada geese. Even with these large pellets, the effective lethal range of steel shot is a little over 40 yards because, unlike lead, velocity drops off dramatically after 40 yards. Problems with barrel damage occurred during initial use of steel shot in shotguns not designed to shoot these very hard pellets. These problems included scoring of the interior of barrels; the most pronounced of these problems was ring-bulging of barrels at the muzzle. When the extra-hard steel shot passed through a traditional full-choke constriction, normally .030 to .045 inches, the hard shot peened the choke and caused that area of the barrel to expand. This expansion normally reached .005 to .015 inch, then stopped. In the case of a single-barrel shotgun, there was only cosmetic damage, but in double-barrel shotguns the bulge caused the barrels to separate. Currently, chokes in the range of .020 constriction (modified choke) or less (improved cylinder, skeet, and even cylinder) can be used with steel shot without barrel damage. If in doubt, a competent gunsmith should be consulted. Currently, high-performance, full chokes with constrictions of .030 to .035 are being manufactured by aftermarket suppliers specifically for use with steel shot. Because steel pellets are so hard and consequently do not deform, they need little choke to ensure tight patterns, although these newer, tighter chokes have proved useful on large geese.

Stevens Arms Company, J. — An arms manufacturer that began operations in Chicopee Falls, Massachusetts, in 1864. In 1920, Savage Arms acquired Stevens and operated as Savage-Stevens for many years, although Savage no longer uses the Stevens name. Between 1877 and 1884, Stevens made a three-triggered shotgun that used the front trigger as an opener. Stevens marketed their own shotguns by model number, but also made side-by-side shotguns for a large contingent of companies that sold the guns under their own private brands. These included: Anniversary Compeer, Aristocrat, Jim Brown, Canadian Industries, Central, Chicago Long Range Wonder, Chicopee Arms, Coast to Coast, Cruso, Diamond Arms Company, Eastern Arms Company, Essex, Falls Arms Company, Hercules, HSB & Company, King Nitro, Knickerbocker, Knockabout, Marshwood, Massachusetts Arms, Monitor Limited, Newport, Olympic, Oxford Arms Company, Paragon, Pioneer Arms Company, Ranger, Riverside Arms Company, Scout, Springfield Arms Company, Sports Champ, Sportsman, Triumph, Tru-Test, Tryon Special, Wittes Hardware Company, and Worthington Hardware Company.

St.-Étienne — The French center of firearm manufacture, and the site of the French proof house. See **proof**.

Stock — 1. The rearmost portion of a shoulder-mounted firearm. 2. A shortening of the term buttstock. See **buttstock, pistol grip, Prince of Wales grip, straight stock**.

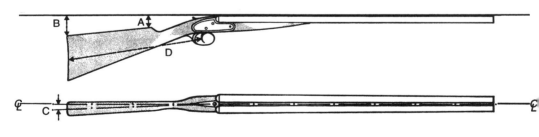

A. Drop at Comb
B. Drop at Heel
C. Cast Off at Heel
D. Length of Pull

Stock: Fitting metal to wood prior to the final fitting and finishing of wood and metal.

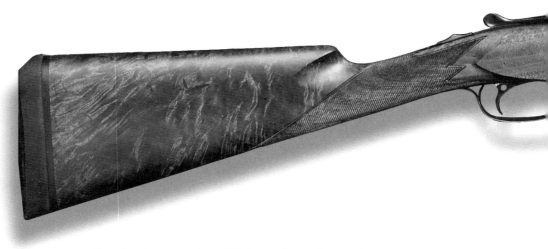

Stock: *An example of high-grade stock wood.*

Stock: *A stocker begins the shaping of a stock using a special clamp to hold the rough stock to the action.*

Stoeger Industries, Inc. — A New York importer of shotguns, rifles, and accessories. Over the years, Stoeger has sold a wide variety of mostly modestly priced shotguns, mainly from Spain and Italy.

Straight stock — A variant of the term "straight hand" or "straight grip," which describes a buttstock with a straight grip area. It is another term for an "English-style" buttstock. See **buttstock, grip.**

Strike — A term that refers to the exterior filing and polishing of the barrels of a shotgun. Other frequently used forms of the word are struck, strike down, strike off, struck down—all referring to the external forming of a barrel.

Striking: *Forming of barrels is called "striking." This workman uses special files to strike the rough barrels to nearly final dimensions.*

Striker (Brit.) — The firing pin, the part of the action that, driven by the force of the tumbler or hammer, actually strikes the primer, igniting the propellant and firing the cartridge. Strikers come in three forms: integral, rebounding, and nonrebounding. Integral strikers are part of the tumbler or hammer and provide fast lock time; only rarely do integral strikers break. Integral strikers are found on the various A. H. Fox shotguns, the Winchester Model 21, the Remington 3200, and elsewhere.

Rebounding strikers are separate strikers within the standing breech and may have a coil spring around them. When the hammer or tumbler hits the rebounding striker it flies forward, impacting the primer and firing the cartridge. However, because the tumbler (or hammer) rebounds slightly, the striker is free to move back from projecting out of the breech face. Semiautomatic and pump-action shotguns employ rebounding strikers or firing pins. The advantage of the rebounding hammer is that it will not continue to push the striker through the breech face, possibly causing difficulty in opening the breech. A nonrebounding hammer moves forward, but, because it does not rebound, the striker remains in the forward position. See **firing pin, hammer, lock time, tumbler.**

Striker: A fully fitted case will contain a striker bottle such as this, made of metal, animal horn, or ivory, to hold a spare set of strikers.

Strozzatura (Ital.) —"Choke."

Sturm, Ruger & Co. — A manufacturer of handguns, rifles, and an over/under shotgun known as the Red Label. Available in a variety of models, the Red Label is currently the only production over/under shotgun that the United States produces. (Remington continues to dabble in over/unders but has not been a factor since the discontinuation of the Model 3200; and Kolar Arms in Wisconsin makes a limited number of competition over/unders primarily for skeet shooters. Galazan makes bespoke over/unders in his Connecticut factory.) A rugged boxlock, the Red Label has inspired few complaints from its users; it is available in a number of configurations, from field to sporting clays.

Suhl, West Germany — One of the major German firearm-producing areas.

Superposed — The trade name given by Browning to their first over/under shotgun.

Sustained lead — One style of leading a moving or flying target. In this style, the shooter swings the gun barrel a given distance in front of the target and maintains that distance while shooting and until the follow-through is complete. In practice, sustained lead is easy to learn, but it is difficult to apply it to a variety of shooting conditions. It is especially useful, however, in skeet shooting. See **lead, swing-through.**

Swamped rib — A rib that is lower at the midpoint than at either the breech or the muzzles, and may be either concave or flat. See **concave rib, rib.**

Swing-through — A style of leading a flying or moving target in which the shooter swings the shotgun from behind the target, establishes the flight path of the target, and then fires as the muzzles swing through or past the target. The gun then continues in a short follow-through. While this style is harder to learn than sustained lead and requires more practice to keep the timing sharp, it is more versatile, being applicable to the entire spectrum of shotgun shooting. See **lead, sustained lead.**

Swivels — Loops that provide a point of attachment for a sling. See **sling.**

Tate, Douglas: *Douglas Tate hunting ducks in Uruguay.*

T

Take-down — A style of shotgun that breaks down into two or more parts for ease of transport and cleaning.

Tampion — A plug for the muzzle of a gun that prevents the entry of dirt or dust. In practice, these also prevent the circulation of air. Because felt baize normally covers the part of the tampion that fits into the muzzle, the tampion is prone to attracting moisture. Tampions can rust into a muzzle, causing severe damage.

Tar-Hunt Custom Rifles, Inc.
— A manufacturer of custom shotguns for shooting sabot slugs at big game. Tar-Hunt, which is in Bloomsburg, Pennsylvania, builds a bolt-action shotgun and modifies pump-action and semiautomatic shotguns for precision shooting with sabot slugs. These shotguns, which hunters use mainly for white-tailed deer, are capable of accuracy comparable to that of a centerfire rifle. See **rifling, sabot, slug.**

Tate, Douglas — Now a resident of Seattle, Washington, Douglas Tate was born and educated in Great Britain and worked in London; Sydney, Australia; and New York prior to settling in the Northwest. An authority on British-made shotguns, Tate is the author of several books on the subject, such as *British Gun Engraving* and *Birmingham Gunmakers*, and is a frequent contributor to sporting publications in the United States and England. He also operates a company that imports British shotguns for sale to knowledgeable clients in the United States.

Temperature — Temperature affects the burning rate of various propellants, and consequently the velocity of the projectile. Although these variations are not sufficient to cause concern, propellants that burn extremely slowly and spherical or ball propellants, which are harder to ignite than flake propellants, may not always burn completely at very cold temperatures.

10-gauge — A shotgun whose bore measures 0.775 inch. Gunmakers originally chambered the 10-gauge for 2 5/8-inch shells, although the current chamber length is 3½ inches. As such, the current 10-gauge is a specialist's shotgun that some hunters prefer for Canada goose and turkey hunting. These shotguns were once available solely as single- or double-barrel shotguns, but since the 1970s three semiautomatics—the Ithaca Mag-10, the Remington SP-10, and the Browning Gold—have been in gun shops; the Browning and Remington are still in production, along with the Browning BPS pump in 10-gauge. However, with the advent and manufacture of several 12-gauge shotguns that take 3½-inch shells, the 10-bore is again declining in sales.

Third bite — See **third fastener**.

Third grip — See **third fastener**.

Third fastener — A third fastener may take many forms, including Greener crossbolt, Purdey concealed fastener, Rigby-Bissel rising bite, Westley Richards doll's head rib

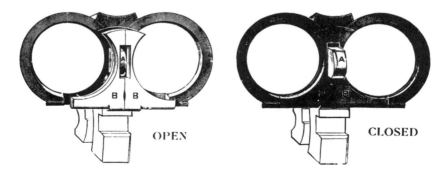

OPEN   CLOSED

extension with a bite, Scott square crossbolt, and Webley screw grip. All of them serve the same purpose by securing the barrels to the action with a third device, the first two being the Purdey underbolt, which consists of a bite in each of the barrel lumps. See **action, balls, bites, crossbolt, Purdey underbolt, Rigby-Bissel rising bite.**

32-gauge — An obsolete shotgun gauge whose bore diameter is 0.526 inch.

36-gauge — An obsolete shotgun gauge whose bore diameter is 0.506 inch.

Thomas, Gough — See **Garwood, Thomas G.**

Thomlinson Cleaner — A type of cleaning device for shotgun bores that used a fine bronze gauze tightly drawn over a pair of slides. Two slides fitted into a carrier that threaded to the tip of a cleaning rod. The manufacturer intended this cleaner to fit into the bore tightly, allowing the fine gauze to scrape away powder fouling and lead residue without the danger of scratching. Replacement slides were available when the originals wore out. Although a good idea, the Thomlinson Cleaner seemed no more useful in practice than did less expensive bronze bore brushes.

Thorn, H. A. A. — The patent holder (1881) for a four-barrel shotgun that Lancaster later built.

Three-barrel guns — Shotguns with three barrels horizontally aligned. Such firms as Dickson, E. C. Green, and Westley Richards made and sold them. Don't confuse them with Continental and especially Austrian and German three-barrel guns that normally incorporated two shotgun barrels and one rifle barrel. See **combination gun, drilling.**

Thumb hole (Brit.) — **1.** The area of the buttstock where the top of the hand or grip rises to form the front top of the comb. **2.** An early underlever-style action by Purdey. It used a lever whose hinge was in front of the trigger guard. The shooter operated it by pushing down on the lever through a hole in the bottom front of the enlarged trigger guard.

Tiro a tiro (Sp.) — "Semiautomatic."

Toe — The bottommost part of a gunstock, where it meets the butt. This part of the buttstock is the lowest contact point with the shooter's shoulder, and it is most important that its length and cast carefully match the shooter's physique. More often than not, the toe of the stock may be too long and pointed for women shooters. Similarly, men with large pectoral muscles will find a long, sharp, pointed toe painful. See **buttstock, gun fit.**

Top lever – The top lever originally derived from the invention of the Scott spindle in 1865. Nearly all contemporary double shotguns open by means of a top lever.

Top strap — The rear projection of a double gun's action. The top strap runs back from the rear of the action into the wrist of the buttstock. It normally contains the safety catch—which often, in the case of a single-trigger gun, includes the barrel selector—and top lever. In the case of large-bore shotguns, and most especially double rifles, the top strap may extend farther back, running up onto the comb of the stock as extra reinforcement. See **action, buttstock, top lever.**

Topperwein, Adolph, and Elizabeth "Plinky" — The husband and wife team of trick-shot artists who represented the Winchester Repeating Arms Company, touring the United States, Canada, and Mexico during the first half of the twentieth century. Elizabeth "Plinky" Topperwein, an excellent shot in her own right, died on January 2, 1945, and following her death Adolph never shot another exhibition; Winchester nevertheless kept him on the payroll until 1951. Adolph Topperwein died near San Antonio, Texas, on March 4, 1962.

Trademark — The name of a shotgun's maker. Manufacturers stamp it onto the barrels and sometimes onto the action.

Trade name — Unlike a trademark, which reflects the maker's name, a trade name is only a name and provides no indication of the actual maker. Trade names appear frequently, especially on old double-barrel, exposed-

Topperwein, Adolph, and Elizabeth "Plinky": *Exhibition shooters Adolph ("Ad") and "Plinky" (Mrs.) Topperwein in 1912.*

hammer shotguns and often those with Damascus barrels. Now-defunct companies like Crescent Arms and especially H. & D. Folsom Arms of New York imported large numbers of these shotguns, which they wholesaled to independent sporting goods, hardware, and chain hardware stores; all bore either house-brand names or other names. By and large, all such shotguns came from factories in Belgium, although some may have come from the large Birmingham gun trade. None bear any great monetary worth today, having, at best, only sentimental value.

Trapshooting — Originating in England, trapshooting began with the shooting of live pigeons. Called "old hats" by the shooters, early pigeon shoots indeed used old top hats to hold the pigeons. An official seated behind the shooter tipped the hat by means of a string. As the sport became more sophisticated, box traps took the place of hats. Ultimately, trapshooting transitioned through shooting feather-filled glass balls to the clay targets in use today.

Trapshooting: *A squad of five shooters engaged in shooting 16-yard traps.*

Conventional 16-yard trapshooting employs a single trap that moves from side to side, presenting targets at random angles to the shooters. A squad consists of five shooters, one on each of five shooting positions a measured 16 yards to the rear of the low traphouse. Each in turn shoots one shot at each target until all have fired five shots. At that time the scorer calls out, "Walk," and each shooter moves one position to the right. The shooter on position five at the far right walks behind the squad to the vacated position one on the far left, and shooting resumes. A target from which a visible piece breaks off counts as a hit or dead target. Any target from which the referee does not see a piece fly off counts as lost.

Handicap trap is very much the same as 16-yard trap, with the exception that shooters stand at varying distances from the traphouse, based on their ability and previous scores. Normally, handicap distances range from 20 to 27 yards. The range for trap doubles is 16 yards, but two targets go up at the same moment. A version of international-style trap, which approximates Olympic-style trap, is automatic trap. This employs a trap that oscillates both back and forth and up and down, approximating the targets a shooter sees when firing over a true Olympic trench.

The shotguns used by shooters for trapshooting are perhaps the most exacting of any for clay target or field-shooting. A trap gun for 16-yard trap can be a repeater, a double-barrel, or a single-barrel gun, normally with modified, improved modified, or full choke. The more open choke is often desirable, as it gives the shooter a wider pattern. Handicap guns normally employ full or extra-full choke, as the distances to the targets are often great. Some handicap guns have custom chokes that provide maximum pattern concentration at the distance at which the shooter consistently fires at handicap targets.

Shotguns for doubles and automatic trap must be capable of firing two shots. Normally over/under or gas-operated semiautomatics are the choice for these variations. Over/unders use modified and full or extra full chokes, and semiautomatics use improved modified or full. See **clay target, Olympic trap, pull.**

Trench — See **Olympic trap.**

Trench gun — A military-style shotgun with a short barrel, for use in a confined space such as a trench. In extensive use in the trench warfare of World War I, repeating shotguns such as the Winchester Models 97 and 12—fitted with a hand guard and bayonet stud and finished with a Parkerized finish—saw heavy service. Shotguns have been important in every conflict since, especially so in Vietnam's jungles. See **Parkerizing.**

Trigger — The link between the shooter's finger and the firing mechanism of the shotgun. See **double triggers, single trigger.**

Trigger group — The portion of a shotgun that when disassembled holds the trigger, sears, and tumblers or hammers. Trigger-plate style shotguns and repeaters have their trigger groups built as one unit. See **droplock.**

Trigger guard — The loop of steel that surrounds the trigger or triggers of a firearm. The guard prevents the accidental pulling of the triggers by brush or other objects, and it provides a resting place for the finger prior to engaging the trigger for a shot. Trigger guards on repeating shotguns often carry the safety catch. On high-grade double guns, the trigger guard will be thicker on the side of the shooter's trigger finger, so that it provides a comfortable resting place for the trigger finger. See **beaded trigger guard, trigger.**

Trigger lock — A device that locks around the trigger and trigger guard, making the intentional firing of the firearm impossible. Available as conventional keyed locks or as electronically operated devices, these locks disable the firearm to protect against accidental discharge or unauthorized use.

Trigger-plate locks — The third style of double shotgun—the other two being the sidelock and boxlock. In this style of shotgun, the locks, including the sear and hammer or tumbler and the triggers, are on the trigger plate. Classic trigger plate guns are Dickson and MacNaughton. A modern variation is the Italian-made Perazzi. On the Perrazi one can push a release lever or catch, and the shooter can drop the locks, or remove them through the bottom of the action. See **Blitz action, drop lock.**

Trigger pull — The feel of, and the weight necessary to move, the trigger as it lifts the sear out of engagement with the sear notch to fire the gun. Gunsmiths measure trigger pull with a scale, and pull should "break"—disengage the sear—at around three to five pounds. The trigger pull for the rear trigger of a double-trigger shotgun is normally heavier by half a pound than for the front trigger, to prevent the second barrel from firing through the effects of recoil. Because the shooter of a shotgun does not squeeze the trigger but instead slaps it, the feel of the pull is not as critical. However, an excessively hard trigger pull, one with a great deal of preliminary take-up or slack, or one that is rough, will tend to be a distraction to the shooter; a competent gunsmith can and should correct such problems. Trigger adjustment, especially to the single trigger of a double gun, is work that is well left only to the most experienced of gunsmiths; home repairs can prove dangerous.

Trigger shoe — A machined-steel or aluminum device that slips over the trigger of a single-trigger shotgun and is secured by means of a small setscrew. In use primarily by clay target shooters, the shoe makes the surface of the trigger where the finger contacts it much wider.

Trio — A set of three matched shotguns for driven game shooting. Prominent figures in game shooting around the turn of the twentieth century such as the Earl de Grey and King Edward VII used these three-gun garnitures. See **composed pair, garniture, matched pair, true pair.**

True pair — Two shotguns with consecutive serial numbers, customarily of side-by-side construction but more recently over/unders, that the gunmaker built at the same time to the exact same stock dimensions, overall weight, barrel length, balance, and often choke. The stocks are built from one double-thick stock blank or fletch. Such guns are primarily for shooting driven game birds. Occasionally, guns of a true pair may have different chokes. In that case, gun number one normally has either a modified or full choke in the right barrel, with cylinder in the left. The second gun of the pair will then have cylinder or improved cylinder in the right barrel and modified or full choke in the left. In practice, the hunter fires the first gun at the approaching birds, the first shot farther away and the second close to the gun. Then the hunter exchanges guns and uses the second gun first to shoot at the close, departing birds and then, using the left barrel, to fire at the last of the birds. Such a pair of shotguns normally share a case, and as a rule the two are indistinguishable from each other in both feel and appearance, save for the gold-inlaid numbers, 1 and 2, that identify each gun.

Often owners of pairs split them, perhaps putting one up for sale. Since the number of true pairs is small, it is often possible to find a gun from a broken pair, and there are individuals who specialize in looking for them. Although pairs normally have consecutive serial numbers, the guns of some pairs do not, the gunmaker having produced these years apart. In that instance, even though the original maker made the second shotgun of the pair to the specifications of the first, these are not a true pair but rather a matched pair. See **composed pair, fletch, matched pair.**

Trunnions — Rounded projections on the inner sides of the action that engage mating cuts in the barrels and around which the barrels pivot. Perhaps the foremost user of this style of hinging, which is unique to over/under shotguns, is Beretta. Trunnions do not require a hook on the barrel lumps and therefore enable the gun designer to make an over/under with a very shallow receiver. The barrels thus can sit quite low in the receiver, thereby directing the recoil more to the rear where the heavy muscles of the upper torso can absorb it.

Try gun — A side-by-side or over/under shotgun whose articulated stock adjusts through a wide range so as to enable a skilled gun fitter to adjust it to an individual shooter during a gun-fitting session. While some feel that the try gun is ill-balanced because of the weight of the adjusters, in the hands of an experienced shooting instructor or fitter it is a most useful tool. See **fitting, pattern board.**

Try gun: This Holland & Holland try gun, with its infinite adjustments, can fit a buttstock to virtually anyone. However, a skilled fitter is absolutely necessary for maximum accuracy.

Tube — **1.** The basic cylindrical, forged barrel prior to reaming or boring, striking, finishing, and jointing. **2.** A term that

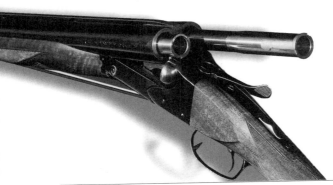

Tube: Small-gauge tubes like these by Briley Manufacturing, Houston, Texas, can quickly convert a larger gauge to a smaller gauge. Favored by skeet shooters and sporting clays shooters, they can also be used for game shooting and hunting.

sometimes refers to a finished barrel, or style of shotgun, such as "twin-tubed." **3.** A casual term for a screw-in choke tube or full-length gauge conversion tube.

Tubular magazine — A tube running beneath the barrel of a repeating shotgun that contains a follower and spring. The spring exerts pressure against the rounds in the magazine so that they will exit at the proper time in the cycling of the gun's mechanism. The follower caps the spring and rests against the head of the last round in the magazine, providing a smooth surface against which the round rests. See **follower, magazine.**

Tumbler (Brit.) — "Hammer." See **hammer.**

Tungsten/polymer shot — A newly developed nontoxic shot with immense potential. Manufacturers produce it by adding specific quantities of micro-fine tungsten powder to a polymer slurry, then casting or injection molding the pellets. By varying the tungsten content, the maker can adjust the density and weight of the pellets so that they duplicate the ballistics of lead shot. In addition to the shot's nontoxic composition and favorable ballistics, because of the elasticity of the pellets they are safe for use in any shotgun capable of firing modern, smokeless-powder ammunition. In 1999, Kent Cartridge and Federal Cartridge Company offered cartridges loaded with tungsten/polymer shot. See **nontoxic shot.**

Turkey gun — A very tightly choked shotgun of 10- or 12-gauge that hunters use for hunting the American wild turkey. Normally these shotguns have a matte-black or camouflage finish to blend with the spring forest. Although any full-choked shotgun will do, the modern turkey gun has a choke that shoots very tight patterns of No. 4 or No. 6 lead shot. Many have either a ghost-ring rear sight or a holographic or red-dot sight to ensure accurate placement of the shot in the head and neck of the turkey. See **ghost-ring sight, red-dot sight.**

Turkey load — A heavily charged shotshell of No. 4 or No. 6 lead shot specifically for hunting American wild turkeys. Normal loading puts up to two ounces of shot into a 3-inch, 12-gauge magnum shell. In combination with a full or extra-full choke, these heavy loads of relatively small pellets can quickly anchor a turkey.

Turnscrew (Brit.) — See **screwdriver.**

12-gauge — The most common shotgun gauge in the world. The 12-gauge offers the shooter the choice of shooting anything from very light to very heavy, magnum loads, along with easy availability of ammunition. A 12-gauge shotgun with interchangeable, screw-in choke tubes is as close to an all-round, go-anywhere, shoot-anything shotgun as can be made. See **gauge.**

12-20 — A gun devised in the late 1800s by the London gunmaker Joseph Lang. His goal was to produce a game gun with better balance. To achieve it, Lang drastically narrowed the barrels of the traditional game gun as they reached the muzzles. Specifically, he narrowed the bore from a 12-gauge to between that of a 16- and a 20-gauge, thereby achieving slim tubes that moved the balance back between the hands. Keeping in mind that British ammunition has always been of lower pressure, one can assume that the gradual narrowing of the bore coupled with lower initial pressures kept these guns safe.

20-gauge — This 0.615-inch-bore shotgun is the choice of many for upland bird hunting. It is one of the four gauges in skeet competition, and with its 7/8- and 1-ounce loads it is effective for most game. Although 20-gauge shotguns chambered for 3-inch shells might seem to be the answer to the all-round shotgun, the sometimes erratic and often poor performance of 3-inch loads at the patterning board and on game quickly proves that idea false.

28-gauge — Of 0.550-inch-bore diameter, this is perhaps the most useful of all the small gauges, including the 20-gauge. Built on a light, appropriately sized frame, these shotguns possess superb handling and pointing characteristics, and the ¾-ounce shot charge is sufficient for grouse, partridge, and quail, for which the 28-gauge is an admirable choice. Under close-flushing conditions, such as when shooting released birds on game farms, the 28-gauge is more than enough for pheasant.

The 28-gauge owes its current existence to the game of skeet, being one of the four shotgun gauges in use in that competition; that alone has kept this gauge alive. Often overlooked in favor of the heavier 20-gauge, the 28-gauge is more than a match for the 20. However, because ammunition sales are slow in this gauge, the variety of commercially available ammunition is meager. But as long as shells are available with No. 6, 7½, 8, and 9 shot, the 28-gauge will remain a primary choice for the upland hunter. See **skeet.**

24-gauge — An obsolete shotgun gauge that fit between the 20- and 28-gauge and whose bore diameter is 0.579. Although no ammunition company commercially loads cartridges for the 24-gauge, brass hulls are available for handloaders.

Twist barrel — See **Damascus barrel.**

Two-inch 12-gauge — A number of light, extremely well-balanced 12-gauge shotguns that were chambered for a 2-inch shell were available at one time from several of the great London and Birmingham gunmakers, such as Charles Lancaster. Almost all predated World War II; makers offered the shotgun primarily as a gun for ladies or young persons. Very lightweight, they swing beautifully.

It is possible to handload shells for these guns by cutting hulls to the proper 2-inch length, and reliable loading data is available in the *Hodgdon Shotshell Data Manual* and elsewhere. In the very late 1990s, some of the Spanish gunmakers began offering side-by-sides chambered for 2-inch shells as a part of their line.

Under hammer — A style of percussion action in which the hammers are under the action.

Underbolt — A sliding locking bolt within the bar of the action or, in the case of an over/under, at the bottom of the action. James Purdey first developed the underbolt, and it has become the standard method of locking the barrels to the action for both side-by-side and over/under shotguns. The underbolt itself is a hardened rectangular piece of steel pierced in two places that engage the bites or locking recesses on the barrel lumps. Although many shotguns that use underbolt lockups have additional crossbolts and third fasteners, they are superfluous, as the sliding underbolt is extremely strong and not in need of further strengthening. See **bites, lump, third fastener.**

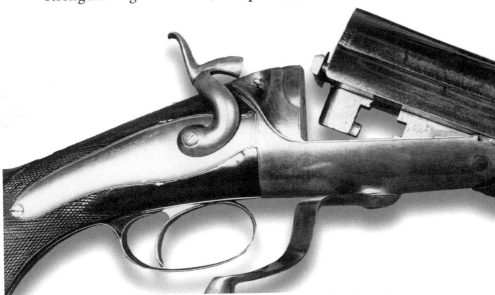

Underlever: The gunmaker designed this single-barrel, four-bore back-action underlever shotgun as a waterfowl gun that the shooter would fire from the shoulder. Of note is the back-action lock—the hammer spring being behind the hammer or tumbler—and the double-grip underlever.

U

Underlever — An early opening device that used a lever under the trigger guard to open the action. One of the earliest was the Jones underlever. With the development of the snap action, gunmakers produced a lever that the shooter pushed down to open the action; upon closing, the underlever, like the more modern top lever, snapped shut. The underlever appeared in several forms, from the thumbhole (a lever just in front of the trigger guard that the shooter pushed through a large, flared hole in the trigger guard) to a lever that folded flush to the trigger guard. See **Jones underlever, snap action.**

Underlugs — Another term for bites or locking recesses. See **bites.**

Universal extractor — A handheld device that shooters used to extract a stuck shotshell. Since the advent of plastic hulls, these have fallen into disuse, but in the days of paper hulls, which could swell in damp weather, a brass extractor that slipped over the head of a stuck shell was a part of every shooter's kit. Many extractors also employed a hook at one end for reaching into the chamber to remove the paper section of the hull should the brass head pull off. See **extractor.**

Upland game — Game birds and small-game animals of the uplands. Birds include the American wild turkey; bobwhite and other quail; pheasant; grouse, Hungarian and red-legged or chukar partridge, and woodcock. Animals include squirrel, rabbit, and hare. See **partridge, quail, rabbit.**

Upland game gun — Any lightweight shotgun choked no tighter than modified. Currently, upland hunters prefer over/unders or sometimes a side-by-side, although some of the more lightweight, 20-gauge semiautomatics are popular. When pheasants are the main bill of fare, the 12-gauge is the first choice, often choked full when hunting long cornfields where roosters may flush in excess of thirty-five yards. For generations the 16-gauge was the upland gun of choice, but sagging ammunition sales and the lack of a manufacturer producing the 16 have nearly driven it from the scene. Still, some prefer the 16-gauge as an all-round upland gun, and many vintage A. H. Foxes, Parkers, and other 16-gauge shotguns are still in use.

Although the 20-gauge is very popular for upland hunting, the 28-gauge is also an excellent choice. Shooting nearly the same shot charge as the 20-gauge, the 28 is lighter and is an extremely fine performer on upland game. Most upland hunters use improved cylinder choke, although a double gun that is choked modified and improved cylinder is about as versatile a shotgun for upland hunting as you can get. Other possibilities are cylinder and full, or improved cylinder in both barrels. With the current availability of interchangeable, screw-in choke tubes, the hunter can now choose the right choke for every cover.

Upland load — Shotshells for the taking of upland birds and animals. For squirrels and rabbits, hunters frequently use field loads of No. 4, 5, or 6 lead shot, the same loads that are in common use for pheasants, whether the hunter shoots from behind dogs or when walking cover without dogs. Because of the ability of pheasants to run ahead and flush at long yardage, very heavy loads are desirable. For the prince of the uplands, the bobwhite quail, it's best to shoot light loads of No. 7½ or 8 lead shot, loads that can also be appropriate for grouse and partridge. Most hunters use the 12-gauge, and although somewhat forgotten, the 16-gauge remains a prime choice for all upland game. Except for bringing down wide-flushing pheasants, the 20- and 28-gauges are both reliable upland gauges.

V-springs: *Sometimes called leaf springs, these V-spings are used in sidelock shotguns.*

Velocity: *Velocity is measured by means of a chronograph such as this one manufactured by PACT. The shot charge or, in the case of a rifle, the projectile, flies through the openings created by the arched plastic diffusers. Beneath each diffuser is a highly sensitive photoelectric cell. When the shot cluster crosses the first photocell it turns the chronograph on, and when the light is interrupted by the shot charge crossing the second cell, the circuit is turned off. The computer then calculates the velocity at which the charge crossed the two cells and displays the result on the screen in feet per second or meters per second, depending on how the computer is programmed.*

V-spring — A type of spring in common use in sidelock-style double shotguns. The V-spring is a folded strip of metal in the shape of a V. A few modern sidelocks employ coil springs because of their durability and low cost. Many believe that V-springs provide smoother trigger pulls and quicker lock time than coil springs, but they are more likely to break. See **springs.**

Val Trompia — The major firearms manufacturing region of Italy.

Velocity — The measurement of the speed of a projectile or, in the case of a shotshell, projectiles. The most frequent velocity reference is at the muzzle. From that velocity, one can predict downrange velocities by using tables or computer programs.

Velocity is all-important in comparing shells and the expectations a hunter can have from various loads. Muzzle velocities of less than 1,000 feet per second (fps) are suitable for skeet and close-flushing upland game such as quail. At 1,150 to 1,200 fps are the target loads and upland game loads. Velocities of 1,250 to 1,300 fps are appropriate for heavy game loads. Currently, steel shot travels at 1,300 to 1,450 fps, in order to provide effective downrange velocity.

Although velocity information is important for comparing shells, it is important to remember that published velocities in ammunition manufacturers' catalogs are the results of tests run under ideal temperatures—65 to 70 degrees Fahrenheit—with 30-inch barrels for the 12-gauge. In shorter or ported barrels, especially in colder weather, velocities will not match published data. Nevertheless, velocity and patterning remain the best tools for evaluating the appropriateness of shotshells for a given task. See **pattern.**

Vena contracta (Latin) — A contracted passage. See **12-20.**

Vented breech — A method of venting propellant gases away from the shooter in the event of a primer or case failure. In one design, there is a concentric groove around the firing pin or striker holes in the standing breech. Intersecting this groove is another groove, one that is horizontal and parallel with the plane of the action bar, ending at the edge of the action balls. Other methods for venting gases include the cutting of shallow lines in the standing breech. If the firing pin pierces the primer, or the primer otherwise fails, the hot gases would follow these grooves to the outside of the action. See **gas vent valve.**

Ventilated rib — A rib running the length of a shotgun barrel that attaches by means of a series of posts or pillars so that air can circulate between the barrel and the rib. Because of the resultant cooling effect, heat mirage is less of a problem during the rapid firing of a large number of shells, especially in hot weather. Furthermore, the ventilated rib provides a flat, matte surface that maintains eye alignment. See **rib.**

Vintagers — A U.S. group that holds a yearly target competition (the Vintage Cup) in which the participants use only side-by-side shotguns or rifles, many of which are hammer guns.

Vierling — A German combination gun with four barrels. See **combination gun.**

Vorderschaft (Ger.) — "Fore-end."

Vorders chaft-Repetier (Ger.) — "Pump action."

Vintagers: *The Vintage Cup is held each year in various locations, mostly in the United States. At this very traditional event, the shooters use side-by-side guns, either shotguns or rifles. Many shooters dress in Edwardian or Victorian outfits. Shown here is Ludo Wurfbain, the 1999 winner of the Dangerous Game Rifle competition.*

Wads: These fiber wads were used to load all shotshells prior to the advent of the all-plastic wad in the 1960s. In some instances these wads are loaded in contemporary shotshells where there are ecological or appearance concerns with plastic wads.

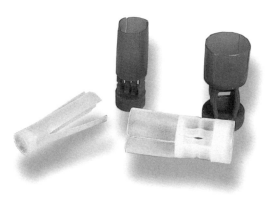

Wads: Contemporary all-plastic wads.

Wads — The material that separates the propellant from the shot charge. The wad or wads serve three purposes: to seal the hot, expanding propellant gases behind the shot charge; to cushion the shot to prevent or minimize distortion; and to take up space within the hull.

Originally, wads for muzzleloading shotguns simply kept the powder and shot separate and the shot from rolling out the muzzle. However, with the development of breechloading cartridges it became evident that the propellant gases had to remain sealed behind the shot charge. Using the hard over-powder card wads of the day, shooters discovered that if the wad column were longer, there would be less chance of the hot gases invading the shot. Further research led to Western-Winchester's development of the Super-Seal cup wad, which is still in use in some of their shotshells. This treated cardboard wad formed a dome over the powder charge and, regardless of the forcing cone or barrel dimensions, could expand to seal in the propellant gases, resulting in higher velocities.

With the increased research into and use of plastics following World War II, pliable but tough polyethylene took the place of cardboard. Along with this came the revelation that wrapping the shot—remember that only lead shot was then in use—in a polyethylene wrapper like the Western-Winchester Mark-5 would protect it, resulting in denser patterns and fewer deformed pellets. Finally both shot protector and gas seal came together in the first one-piece all-plastic Remington Power Piston wad.

With the requirement for nontoxic shot in waterfowl hunting, new challenges arose. The gas seal was available, but now the problem for the shot was the reverse. With lead shot the problem is to protect the soft shot from deformation resulting from contact with the barrel; now the challenge was to protect the barrel from the hard steel shot. The use of thicker and tougher plastics ultimately resolved this problem.

Walsingham, 6th Lord (1843–ca. 1915) — A contemporary of the Earl de Grey (also known as Lord Ripon), King Edward VII, and his son (who became King George V). No less a fine shot than Lord Ripon considered Walsingham the finest game shot of his day. In 1903, *Bailey's* magazine listed the twelve best game shots in England. Lord Ripon was first and Walsingham third, with a Mr. R. H. Rimington Wilson (whom many thought an odd choice) coming in second. Although Walsingham was a crack shot, his finances were not up to the level necessary to sustain his shooting career, and he spent his later years abroad.

There is an oft-repeated story regarding the shooting abilities of both Lords Ripon and Walsingham. Rules that all must follow govern driven game shooting; if one fails to respect the rules,

Walsingham, 6th Lord:
The 6th Lord Walsingham was considered one of the five best shots in England at the turn of the twentieth century.

"One will blot their copy book and not be asked to return," to quote the late shooting instructor and gunmaker Robert Churchill. On one occasion the two men were at Lord Ripon's pheasant shoot in Yorkshire, and a covey of partridge flushed over the two marksmen. Again quoting Churchill: "The standard of etiquette in shooting in the nineteenth century was exemplified in the story of Lord Walsingham and Lord Ripon . . . [who] were surprised by a covey of eight partridges which swept overhead of them in the middle of a pheasant drive. Immediately the two men fired two barrels, changed guns, and fired another two barrels into the covey. Between them they shot the lot. The story was quoted in their own time, not for the brilliance of their feat in bringing down four birds each out of the covey, but for the fact they were so experienced, and they knew the etiquette of shooting so perfectly that neither of them shot at what might have been counted the other's bird."

Waterfowl — Ducks and geese generally. Subgroups consist of the dabbling and diving species, and sea ducks.

Water table — Another term for the bar of the action. See **bar, breakoff**.

Weatherby, Inc. — An arms maker famous for their high-velocity, magnum-caliber rifles, Weatherby also imports over/under,

Weatherby, Inc.: Weatherby makes over-and-under and semiautomatic shotguns. The over-and-under shotguns come in two models, Orion and Athena, both of which have several grades. Shown here is an Athena III grade.

pump-action, and semiautomatic shotguns from Japan. Of consistently good quality, these guns nevertheless suffer in the marketplace because of consumers' association of the Weatherby name solely with rifles.

Weight — Gun weight is a rather subjective subject, although Greener's rule of ninety-six provides a good guideline. What feels good to a six-foot-four-inch athlete will be too heavy for a petite woman. However, too light a shotgun is a boon to no one.

It is important to point out that while weight is important, balance is perhaps more important. British-made 12-gauge shotguns chambered for two-inch shells are extremely light yet have superb balance; they therefore do not feel too light. In general, a double 12-gauge 6¼ to 7 pounds, a 16-gauge about the same, a 20-gauge double can hover at the 6-pound mark, and a 28 can go 5½ pounds. Shotguns for waterfowling must of necessity be heavier, lest they pound the shooter and themselves into oblivion. A 12-gauge double for waterfowl should weigh no less than 8 pounds, and a 10-bore ought to tip the scales at at least 10 pounds; the 3½-inch 12-gauge ought to also, but they don't. Shotguns for clay target shooting benefit from both weight and longer barrels, the latter supplying some heft. Most shooters now find that longer barrels combined with added weight provide the steadiest and smoothest swing.

If a shotgun is not heavy enough, the shooter can add weight to the forearm, buttstock, or both. The random addition of weight in and of itself is not recommended, however, as added weight must not alter the gun's balance. Shooters often rout a cavity in the bottom of their fore-end and fill it with a lead shot/glue mixture. Drilling holes into the buttstock for the same shot/glue mixture can also be of help. See **balance, Greener's rule of ninety-six.**

Weight of game — The following are the weights of various upland game and waterfowl:

Species	Weight
Grouse	1 to 1¾ pounds
Mallard duck	2 to 3 pounds
Partridge	13 to 15 ounces
Pheasant	2½ to 3½ pounds
Quail	3 to 4 ounces
Rabbit	2½ to 3½ pounds
Canvasback duck	3 to 4 pounds
Canada goose and subspecies	4 to 14½ pounds

Westley Richards & Co., Ltd. — Perhaps the most recognizable name in gunmaking in Great Britain, Westley Richards is not, however, a London maker. William Westley Richards established his original factory in the city of Birmingham in 1812, where the company continues today. Westley Richards is well known for producing top-of-the-line shotguns. William Anson and John Deeley, the inventors of the Anson & Deeley boxlock action, were both employees of Westley Richards. Additionally, Deeley and another Westley Richards employee, Leslie B. Taylor, invented and patented the famous droplock action, in which the lockwork is on plates that are removable through the bottom of the action.

Westley Richards continues to make about twenty-five to thirty bespoke shotguns a year. Note that over the history of British gunmaking, there have been about seventeen British gunmakers whose last name was Richards. Also, many inexpensive Belgian-made shotguns have come into the United States under the trade name W. Richards. Westley Richards has never used an abbreviated first name to identify its shotguns.

Wildfowling (Brit.) — Waterfowl hunting.

William Evans, Ltd. — Established in 1883, William Evans continues in business in London, producing a very limited number of bespoke side-by-side and over/under shotguns and an equally small number of double and bolt-action rifles a year.

Williams, David M. "Carbine" — A Winchester Repeating Arms employee whose gas tappet device made possible the M1 carbine, which the military used extensively in World War II and the Korean conflict. In designing the Winchester Models 50 and 59, it was Williams who developed the slip-chamber inertia action. In this type of recoil-operated semiautomatic shotgun, the barrel is solidly fixed to the receiver or action. When a shell fires, the chamber that carries the equivalent of the barrel extension, to which the breechbolt locks, recoils a very short distance. During this short recoil stroke, a heavy inertia block in the buttstock that is linked to the breechbolt starts in motion. It draws the bolt to the rear, unlocking it from the slip chamber and stripping the fired hull from the chamber. The hull ejects when it strikes the ejector stud. At the end of the breechbolt's travel it locks to the rear if the magazine is empty.

If there is a fresh round in the tubular magazine, the breechbolt trips the shell latch, releasing the round from the magazine. The fresh round strikes the bolt release, and the bolt starts forward. By cam action, the carrier raises and aligns the new round with the chamber, and the breechbolt drives forward by means of a spring in the buttstock that had compressed during the opening phase of the cycle. The fresh round moves into the chamber. As the shell's rim stops against the rebate on the face of the chamber, the extractor snaps over the rim, ready to repeat the cycle.

The Model 50 and 59 Winchester semiautomatics had the inertia mechanism in their buttstocks, and consequently they were extremely butt-heavy. They did not possess the balance and handling characteristics of their competitors' semiautomatic shotguns, and they soon faded from the market.

Winchester Repeating Arms Company — Founded in the mid-1800s by Oliver F. Winchester, Winchester primarily made repeating rifles and imported double-barrel shotguns from England, stamping the Winchester name on them. Although Winchester manufactured the Model 1887 lever-action shotgun in both 10- and 12-gauge, the company quickly replaced the Model 1887 with the exposed-hammer slide-action Model 1893. Next came the stronger Model 1897, which the company later renamed the Model 97, and that stayed in production until 1957. In 1912, Winchester introduced their greatest repeating shotgun, the Model 12. Initially a 20-gauge, a 12-gauge quickly followed then the 16-gauge, and ultimately the 28-gauge, the rarest of all Model 12s. The .410 version was the Model 42, and while different in several respects, it still adhered to the lines and function of the Model 12.

In the 1930s, Winchester fell on hard times, primarily because of a foolish expansion into home appliances and other items such as roller skates. Franklin Olin, the owner of Western Cartridge, bought the company at the foreclosure sale in December 1931. Olin cut the manufacturing to strictly firearms, and Winchester continued to produce quality sporting arms. When Olin purchased the Winchester Repeating Arms Company, a side-by-side shotgun was on the drawing board, and Franklin's son John Olin saw to it that the gun came into production as the Model 21. Produced in 12-, 16-, 20-, and 28-gauges, as well as .410-bore, the Winchester Model 21 is, among fine-quality shotguns, without a doubt the strongest, due in part to the very long action bar. Winchester subjected a randomly selected 12-gauge Model 21 to the firing of two thousand proof loads with no noticeable damage. In another instance, one of the Winchester representatives shot hundreds of trap targets with the locking or underbolt removed, simply holding it shut with his forward hand.

Winchester Repeating Arms Company: *Mr. John M. Olin was the driving force behind the production of the Model 21.*

Later Winchester introduced two semiautomatic shotguns, the Models 50 and 59. Based on a short recoiling slip-chamber, both guns were butt-heavy and never caught on with shooters. The ultralight Model 59 was, however, a harbinger of things to come. It used an aluminum receiver and the barrel was a thin steel liner wrapped with fiberglass and bonded with epoxy resin. The muzzle of the Model 59 had threads for the first Winchoke®, the precursor of today's screw-in chokes although not recognized by the firearms industry of 1959 as of potential use for all shotguns.

In 1964, Winchester Repeating Arms Company junked all of the fine firearms that had made them famous, and replaced them with less than stellar guns. Only the Super X Model 1 semiautomatic, which Winchester introduced in the mid-1970s, was a quality shotgun. In spite of its all milled-steel parts, good lines, and reliability, it was more expensive than the competition and too expensive to manufacture; the company dropped it after several years of production. It was not until the 1990s that Winchester—by then named U.S. Repeating Arms Company, which licenses the Winchester name and trademark from the Olin Corporation—began making the kind of firearms for which they are famous. Bought in 1998 by the French conglomerate GIAT, who also own Browning, U.S. Repeating Arms/ Winchester produced the first new Winchester shotgun in decades, a gas-operated semiautomatic called the Super X 2. See **Williams, David A.**

Wind deflection — Just as the wind deflects rifle bullets, so it does shotgun pellets. However, because of the short-range nature of shotgunning, wind deflection is not nearly the problem that it is with solid projectiles at far longer ranges. However, at long shotgun ranges, 40 yards and beyond, pellet drift is a factor, and in some cases a major one. The table on the following page illustrates the effect wind has on shot:

Drift in inches at:	40 yards	50 yards	60 yards	70 yards	80 yards
No. 4 lead	6.56	10.38	15.06	20.71	27.47
No. 4 steel	8.36	13.21	19.28	26.80	35.90

Ten-mile-per-hour crosswind at 90 degrees to the shot column
Courtesy: Winchester Division/Olin Corporation

Wingshooting — A loose term that covers all forms of shooting at flying game birds or clay targets with a shotgun.

Woodcock — A migratory upland bird that frequents the same cover as ruffed grouse. Woodcock most often favor very moist soil, where they drill for earthworms with their long, articulated beak. The woodcock is a plump game bird that flies in a peculiar manner, with its long beak pointing at the ground.

Wood pigeon shooting (Brit.) — These pigeons are an agricultural pest, and farmers encourage hunters to shoot them. Most wood pigeon shooting closely resembles waterfowl hunting. Hunters use decoys, a good hide or blind is a necessity, and, ideally, the birds come in with their wings set much like a decoying duck.

Würgebohrung (Ger.) – "Choke."

Young's .303 — The brand name of a lubricant in extensive use in Great Britain. Although still popular with many British gunsmiths and others, Young's .303 was never a success in the United States, probably because it was virtually impossible to find. Like Rangoon Oil, it has lost out to synthetic lubricants.

ZZ Birds: *ZZ birds are spun into the air by erratically rotating electrical motors hidden behind small screens so the shooter cannot see in which direction the bird will release.*

ZZ Birds: *The ZZ bird consists of two parts, the cup and the wings. When hit, the cup detaches from the wings and the two parts tumble to earth. Often they can be reassembled and used again.*

Z

Zoli, Angelo; Zoli, Antonio — Many relatively inexpensive over/ under shotguns have come into the United States and other countries under the trade name A. Zoli. To the consternation of many, these two Brescia, Italy, manufacturers are separate and distinct, and consequently their shotguns are not interchangeable. To make matters more confused, both used only the initial "A" in their trade name, so it is difficult to differentiate one from the other. Repair parts are not common to either gun. As of 1999, neither shotgun is currently coming into the United States.

Zündhütchen (Ger.) – "Primer."

Zwieling (Ger.) – "Two-barrel gun." See **combination gun.**

Zylinder (Ger.) — "Cylinder."

ZZ Birds — A flying target, incorporating a clay target-shaped center and propeller-like wings, that is launched at great speed. Like a child's spinner, the machine that throws ZZ Birds spins the propellers very fast, from 6,500 to 10,000 rpm, on five small, electrically driven machines that launch the targets at erratic angles. The plastic targets are reusable. Because the plastic targets are recycled, there are no environmental concerns from broken target pieces. Popular in Europe, ZZ Birds now have a fairly large following in the United States, including an association and tournaments. All world-class events are controlled by F.I.T.A.S.C. in Paris, and the universal name of the game is "Helice."

Bibliography

Adams, Cyril S., and Braden, Robert S. *Lock, Stock, and Barrel.* Long Beach: Safari Press, 1996.

Amor, Damián Fermín Vaquero. *Perdices.* Barcelona: Editorial Hispano Europea, S. A., 1983.

Andrews, John. *The Best Shooting in Scotland.* Moffat, Scotland: Lochar Publishing, 1991.

Arnold, Richard. *Automatic and Repeating Shotguns.* New York: A. S. Barnes Company, 1958.

Baer, Larry L. *The Parker Gun.* North Hollywood: Bienfield Publishing, 1980.

Bauer, Erwin A. *The Duck Hunter's Bible.* Garden City: Doubleday & Company, 1965.

Beaumont, Richard. *Purdey's: The Guns and the Family.* London: David & Charles, 1984.

Begbie, Eric, and Humpreys, John. *The Beacon Shooting Buyer's Guide.* Wellingboro, England: Beacon Publishing, 1986.

Bellrose, Frank C. *Ducks, Geese & Swans of North America.* Harrisburg: Stackpole Books, 1976.

Black, James F. *Black's Wing and Shot Shotgunner's Handbook.* Red Bank: Black's Sporting Directories, 1998.

Bodio, Stephen. *Good Guns.* New York: Nick Lyons Books, 1986.

Boothroyd, Geoffrey. *The Shotgun.* London: A & C Black; Long Beach: Safari Press, 1985.

Boothroyd, Geoffrey. *Shotguns and Gunsmiths.* London: A & C Black; Long Beach: Safari Press, 1986.

Bowlen, Bruce. *The Orvis Wing-Shooting Handbook.* New York: Nick Lyons Books, 1985.

Bowman, Steve, and Wright, Steve. *Arkansas Duck Hunter's Almanac.* Fayetteville: Ozark Delta Press, 1998.

Brister, Bob. *Moss, Mallards & Mules.* New York: Winchester Press, 1969.

———. *Shotgunning: The Art and Science.* New York: Winchester Press, 1976.

Bibliography

British Proof Authorities. *Notes on the Proof of Shotguns & Other Small Arms,* The Worshipful Company of Gunmakers of the City of London and the Guardians of the Birmingham Proof House (The Proof House, 48 Commercial Road, London E1 1LP; The Gun Barrel Proof House, Banbury Street, Birmingham B5 5RH).

Brophy, Lt. Col. William S. *L. C. Smith Shotguns.* North Hollywood: Bienfield Publishing, 1979.

Browning, John, and Gentry, Curt. *John M. Browning: American Gunmaker.* Garden City: Doubleday & Company, 1964.

Buckingham, Nash. *"Mr. Buck": The Autobiography of Nash Buckingham.* Edited by Dyrk Halstead and Steve Smith. Traverse City: Countrysport Press, 1990.

Burrard, Maj. Sir Gerald. *In the Gunroom.* London: Herbert Jenkins, 1930.

Butler, David F. *The American Shotgun.* New York: Winchester Press, 1973.

Buxton, Aubrey. *The King in His Country.* Woodstock: Countryman Press, n.d.

Carder, Charles E. *Recognizing Side-by-side Shotguns.* Delphos: Avil Orize Publishing, 1996.

————. *Side-by-sides of the World.* Delphos: Avil Orize Publishing, 1997.

Churchill, Robert. *Game Shooting.* Revised by MacDonald Hastings. Harrisburg: Stackpole Books, 1971.

————, and Hastings, MacDonald. *Robert Churchill's Game Shooting.* Traverse City: Countrysport Press, 1990.

Connett, Eugene V., ed. *Wildfowling in the Atlantic Flyway.* New York: Bonanza Books, 1949.

————. *Wildfowling in the Mississippi Flyway.* New York: D. Van Nostrand Co., 1949.

Cradock, Chris. *A Manual of Clayshooting.* London: B. T. Bratsford, 1986.

Davies, Ken. *The Better Shot.* London: Quiller Press, 1992.

Evans, George Bird. *The Best of Nash Buckingham.* New York: Winchester Press, 1973.

_____. *Dear John—: Nash Buckingham's Letters to John Bailey.* Old Hemlock: George and Kay Evans, 1984.

_____. *Opus 10: Men Who Shot and Wrote about It.* Old Hemlock: George and Kay Evans, 1983.

_____. *Upland Gunner's Book.* Clinton: Amwell Press, 1979.

_____. *The Upland Shooting Life.* New York: Alfred A. Knopf, 1971.

Fackler, Kurt D., and McPherson, M. L. *Reloading for Shotgunners.* Iola: Krause Publications, 1997.

Fjestad, S. P. *Blue Book of Gun Values.* 19th ed. Minneapolis: Blue Book Publications, 1998.

Garwood, Gough Thomas. *Gough Thomas's Gun Book.* Auburn Hills: Gunnerman Press, 1994.

_____. *Shotgun Shooting Facts.* New York: Winchester Press, 1978.

Grassi, Rodolfo. *El Gran Libro Del Cazador.* Barcelona: Editorial De Vecchi, S. A., 1984.

Greener, W. W. *The Gun and Its Development.* 9th ed., 1910. New York: Bonanza Books.

Gresham, Grits. *The Complete Wildfowler.* New York: Winchester Press, 1973.

_____. *Weatherby: The Man. The Gun. The Legend.* Nachitoches: Cane River Publishing, 1992.

Grozik, Richard S. *Game Gun.* Oskosh: Willow Creek Press, 1986.

Harbour, Dave. *Hunting the American Wild Turkey.* Harrisburg, Pennsylvania: Stackpole, 1975.

Harlan, Howard, and Anderson, W. Crew. *Duck Calls: An Enduring American Folk Art.* Nashville: Harlan Anderson Press, 1988.

Hartman, B. C. (Barney). *Hartman on Skeet.* Toronto: McClelland and Stewart, 1967.

Hastings, MacDonald. *How to Shoot Straight.* New Jersey: A. S. Barnes and Company, 1970.

_____. *The Other Mr. Churchill.* New York: Dodd, Mead & Company, 1965.

————. *The Shotgun.* London: David & Charles, 1983.

Hatch, Alden. *Remington Arms: An American History.* Ilion: Remington Arms Company, 1972.

Hearn, Arthur. *Shooting and Gun Fitting.* London: Herbert Jenkins, n.d. (ca. 1930).

Heilner, Van Campen. *A Book on Duck Shooting.* Philadelphia: Penn Publishing Company, 1939.

Herter's Inc. *Herter's Wholesale Catalog No. 81.* Waseca: Herter's, 1970.

Hightower, John. *Pheasant Hunting.* New York: Alfred A. Knopf, 1946.

Hill, Gene. *A Hunter's Fireside Book.* New York: Winchester Press, 1972.

————. *Mostly Tailfeathers: Stories about Guns and Dogs and Other Odds and Ends.* Piscataway: New Century Publishers, 1974.

Hinman, Bob. *The Duck Hunter's Handbook.* Prescott: Wolf, 1993.

————. *The Golden Age of Shotgunning.* New York: Winchester Press, 1975.

Holmgren, Christer. *Praktiskt Jaktsytte.* Rabén and Sjögren: ICA Bokförlag, 1991.

————. *Vapnet Och Jakten.* Västerås, Sweden: ICA Bokförlag, 1988.

Humphreys, John, ed. *The Shooting Handbook.* Northampton: Beacon Publishing, 1985.

Hughes, Steven Dodd. *Fine Gunmaking: Double Shotguns.* Iola: Krause Publications, 1998.

Jackson, Anthony. *So You Want to Go Shooting.* London: Arlington Books, 1974.

Jeffrey, W. J., & Co. *Jeffrey's Guns, Rifles & General Shooting Accessories.* London: W. J. Jeffrey, 1912-13.

Johnson, Peter H. *Parker: America's Finest Shotgun.* New York: Bonanza Books, 1961.

King, Peter. *The Shooting Field: One Hundred and Fifty Years with Holland & Holland.* London: Quiller Press, 1985.

Knap, Jerome. *All about Wildfowling in America.* New York: Winchester Press, 1976.

Knight, Richard Alden. *Mastering the Shotgun.* New York: E. P. Dutton Co., 1975.

Lancaster, Charles. *The Art of Shooting.* London: McCorquodale & Co., 1954.

Lind, Ernie. *The Complete Book of Trick and Fancy Shooting.* Secaucus: Citadel Press, 1972.

Madis, George. *The Winchester Model Twelve.* Brownsboro: Art and Reference House, 1982.

Marchington, James. *Book of Shotguns.* London: Pelham Books, 1984.

Marcot, Roy. Remington: *The Official Authorized History of Remington Arms Company.* Madison: Remington Arms, 1998.

Marshall-Ball, Robin. *The Sporting Shotgun: A User's Handbook.* Surrey: Saiga Publishing Co., 1982.

Martin, Brian P. *British Game Shooting, Rough Shooting and Wildfowling.* North Pomfret: Trafalger Square Publishing, 1988.

_____. *The Great Shoots.* London: David & Charles, 1987.

Matunas, Edward A. *American Ammo.* Danbury: Outdoor Life Books, 1989.

McCawley, E. S., Jr. *Shotguns & Shooting.* New York: Van Nostrand Reinhold Company, 1965.

McGrath, Brian. *Duck Calls and Other Game Calls.* Plano: Thomas B. Reel Co., 1988.

McIntosh, Michael. *Best Guns.* Traverse City: Countrysport Press, 1989.

_____. *The Best Shotguns Ever Made in America.* New York: Charles Scribner's Sons, 1981.

_____. *More Shotguns and Shooting.* Selma: Countrysport Press, 1998.

_____. *Shotguns and Shooting.* Traverse City: Countrysport Press, 1995.

Missildine, Fred, and Karas, Nicky. *Score Better at Skeet.* New York: Winchester Press, 1972.

Muderlak, Ed. *Parker Guns: The Old Reliable.* Long Beach: Safari Press, 1997.

National Rifle Association of America. *NRA Firearms Fact Book.* Washington, D. C.: National Rifle Association of America, 1989.

———. *Waterfowl Hunting.* Washington, D.C.: National Rifle Association of America, 1988.

———. *Wild Turkey Hunting.* Washington, D.C.: National Rifle Association of America, 1988.

Nichols, Bob. *Skeet: And How to Shoot It.* New York: G. P. Putnam's Sons, 1947.

Nonte, George C., Jr. *Firearms Encyclopedia.* New York: Harper and Row, 1973.

Norman, Geoffrey. *The Orvis Book of Upland Bird Shooting.* New York: Nick Lyons Books, 1985.

Norris, Dr. Charles C. *Eastern Upland Shooting.* Traverse City: Countrysport Press, 1989.

O'Connor, Jack. *The Shotgun Book.* New York: Alfred A. Knopf, 1974.

Popowski, Bert. *Olt's Hunting Handbook.* Pekin: P. S. Olt Company, 1948.

Purdey, T. D. S. and J. A. *The Shotgun.* London: Adam & Charles Black, 1965.

Rose, Michael. *The Eley Book of Shooting Technique.* London: Chancerel Publishers, 1979.

Ruffer, J. E. M. *The Art of Good Shooting.* New York: Drake Publishers, 1972.

Ruffner, Jonathan Garnier. *The Big Shots: Edwardian Shooting Parties.* New York: ARCO Publishing Co., 1977.

Scharff, Robert. *Complete Duck Shooter's Handbook.* New York: G. P. Putnam's Sons, 1957.

Schwing, Ned. *Winchester's Finest: The Model 21.* New York: Krause Publications, 1990.

Smith, A. J. *Sporting Clays.* Wautoma, Wisconsin: Willow Creek Press, 1989.

Stadt, Ronald W. *Winchester Shotguns and Shotshells.* Tacoma: Armory Publications, 1984.

Stanbury, Percy, and Carlisle, G. L. *Shotgun and Shooter.* London: Barrie & Jenkins, 1970.

———. *Shotgun Marksmanship.* Cranbury, New Jersey: A. S. Barnes & Co., 1969.

Stanford, J. K. *The Complex Gun.* London: Pelham Books, 1968.

Tate, Douglas. *Birmingham Gunmakers.* Long Beach: Safari Press, 1997.

Taylor, Zack. *Successful Waterfowling.* New York: Crown Publishers, 1974.

Walker, Ralph T., and Lewis, Jack. *Shotgun Gunsmithing.* Northfield: DBI Books, 1983.

Wallack, L. R. *American Shotguns: Design and Performance.* New York: Winchester Press, 1977.

Wieland, Terry. *Spanish Best: The Fine Shotguns of Spain.* Traverse City: Countrysport Press, 1994.

Willow Creek Press's Editors. *Back Then: A Pictorial History of Americans Afield.* Wautoma, Wisconsin: Willow Creek Press, 1989.

Wood, J. B. *The Gun Digest Book of Firearms. Assembly/Disassembly: Part V: Shotguns.* Northwood: DBI Books, 1980.

Woods, Shirley E. *Gunning for Birds & Wildfowl.* New York: Winchester Press, 1976.

Yardley, Michael. *Gunfitting.* Long Beach: Safari Press, 1993.

Zutz, Don. *The Double Shotgun.* Piscataway: New Century Publishers, 1985.

———. *Modern Waterfowl Guns & Gunning.* South Hackensack: Stoeger Publishing Co., 1985.

Zutz, Don, and Reiber, Ron L. *Hodgdon Powder Company Shotshell Data Manual.* Hodgdon Powder Company, Shawnee Mission, Kansas, 1996.

Periodicals:

The Double Gun Journal (Double Gun Journal, Inc., East Jordan, Mich.)